Mitered Entrelac

Knitting Entrelac Around the Corner

Laura Barker

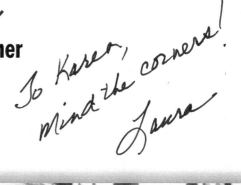

*To Karen,
mind the corners!
Laura*

photography by Tanis Gray

Patterns, charts, diagrams and text ©2014 Laura Barker/CathedralKnits
Photos © 2014 Tanis Gray/TanisKnits and Laura Barker/CathedralKnits
Book Designer: Kim Saar Richardson
Technical Editor: Teresa Halvorson-Fox
Copy Editing, Proofreading: Vicki L. Plaut
Test Knitting: Laura Kosar, Dena Rauch

Cathedral Knits
ISBN: 978-0-69233-961-9
BISAC: Crafts & Hobbies / Needlework / Knitting

TABLE OF CONTENTS

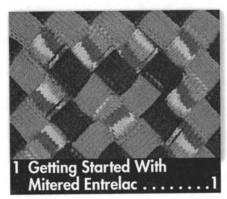

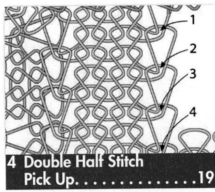

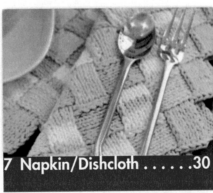

TABLE OF CONTENTS

FOREWORD

The path to knitting mitered entrelac began with an actual journey. In 2012, I was on my way to my first ever knitting convention, hoping to turn years of volunteer knitting, designing and teaching into a new career. En route, I stopped at a friend's house and was intrigued by the mirror in her powder room. Normally, I'm much more drawn to texture, but the colors were so vibrant and appealing that I snapped a picture (Figure 1).

At the convention, one of the sponsors, a yarn producer, asked me to think about designing for her vibrant, appealing yarns, and I immediately thought of the mirror. Several mornings later, I awoke very early thinking of a design for a toddler entrelac cardigan with raglan sleeves using the vibrant colors, and letting the natural shape of the entrelac form a zig zag border at the finished edges. I'd knit toddler cardigans from the neck down, with raglan sleeves in lace or stockinette stitch, and it just seemed logical that entrelac, with its intrinsically rectangular shape, would turn a corner beautifully. The first round went well although it did require some strange blocks, like a rectangle that required picking up stitches down the side of the block just knit for later joining. (Figure 2)

The second round wasn't too bad, with just a couple of strange blocks. (Figure 3)

By round 3, things got even stranger when I had to pick up the stitches for a new rectangle from the short edge of the rectangle in the round below. That result looked like one very long, skinny, two-colored entrelac block. This made it clear that when you turned the raglan corner, the slanting orientation of the entrelac block turned the corner too. (Figure 4)

When standing back a little though, I could see the overall pattern I'd envisioned developing and hoped that the next round would pull that long, skinny rectangle into a shape a bit more square. Unfortunately, the other development was two huge charts, one for left slanting entrelac and one for right, describing how to knit the various blocks. While I was getting a little more comfortable with knitting these non-standard blocks, the task of labeling and clearly describing all of them seemed daunting. Fortunately, after round 4, the raglan yoke was finished and except for a couple of creative triangles under each arm, only standard entrelac rectangles remained to complete the sweater. When the sweater was done, friends in my knitting group and at my local yarn shop, loved the sweater and assured me that the strange blocks and turns at the raglan "corners" were barely noticeable. They were still very noticeable to me, and I was even more worried that all the strange blocks were

FIGURE 1 My friend's mirror

FIGURE 2 First Round Block

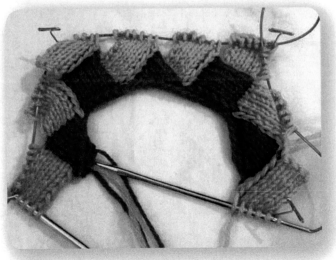

FIGURE 3 Second Round

so tortured and complicated that few would ever persist and knit the sweater.

The next step was to research everything entrelac, in my own library, on the internet, in videos, newer books, even crochet. Crochet entrelac turns the corner, but knit entrelac just didn't. It was either worked in one direction or in the round, with expanding or decreasing blocks. The only way, it seemed, to knit my sweater design without the corner issues, was to work the yoke in a flat piece, in one direction, and then knit the body and sleeves. While this worked well enough for a small sweater, my mind was already dreaming of a baby blanket with rectangular bands of color that looked like rainbow sherbet. For a large, flat piece, changing colors for each entrelac block at the sides would be tedious, but not as tedious as sewing in all the ends! Tortured corners were not what I had in mind either. Finally, I drew a diagram of a blanket, showing the colors, corners, and entrelac direction arrows (Figure 5).

After staring at it many times, and considering possibilities, I had my eureka moment. Each round needed to change colors as it turned the corner, the top and

FIGURE 4 Third Round

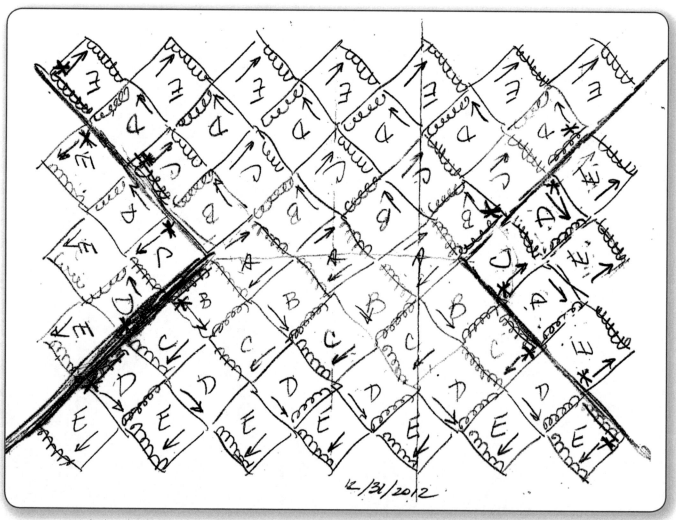

FIGURE 5 First Blanket Sketch

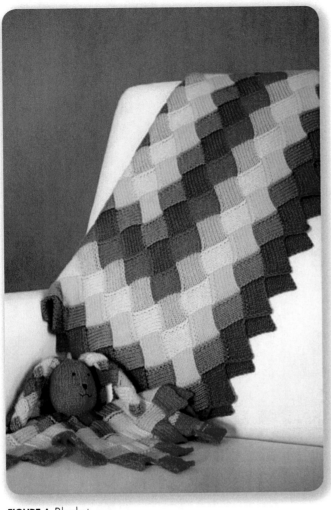

FIGURE 6 Blanket

bottom worked in one color, and the sides in the "next" color. This made all the same color entrelac blocks of each band slant in the same direction. Corners were no longer tortured. Most of the strange blocks went away, and the few remaining ones weren't that strange or difficult to explain. "Pretty" and "easy" are two of my favorite words; this was looking promising. The precision of matching edges at the corners reminded me of building picture frames, so I named this new technique "Mitered Entrelac." After choosing yummy rainbow colors, I knit the blanket. (Figure 6)

As the blanket and my happiness grew, my mind turned to other possibilities of entrelac turning corners. Crochet, harlequin pictures, anything boxy, even shutters on buildings provided inspiration. Most of the patterns in this book are flat and reasonably straightforward. If you've knit entrelac before, this is just a slightly new path. If you haven't knit entrelac before, it's a fun technique, but you might want to try something knit in one direction before turning corners, just like learning to drive. A few of the patterns get more complicated, but I've worked very hard to make the pictures and writing clear and logical to follow. Finally, if you love this expansion of your knitting universe and wonder where else mitered entrelac might lead you, stay tuned.

Most of the patterns in this book will be formed with concentric rectangles, so we will begin with that basic shape. Although you will be forming corners, you will also be working all the way around the rectangle, so each time around the rectangle will be called a round. The direction of work will be called counterclockwise or clockwise. These basic rectangles will begin with a center row (often only one block), worked in only one direction with only one color, and each of these blocks will be provisionally cast on to allow you to work all the way around on your second round. Although you only work in one direction, it will still be called Round 1.

For Round 2 and following rounds, you will begin working around the rectangle, actually working four entrelac tiers; top tier, right side tier, bottom tier, and left side tier, which are joined at the corners. To turn the corners, you will need a special block at the beginning and end of each tier; all the other middle-of-tier blocks will be traditional entrelac blocks. You will change colors when you turn the corners, and break yarn only when you change colors. Similar to traditional entrelac, at the beginning of each round (but not tier), you will change the direction of your work from counterclockwise to clockwise or vice versa.

To get started, we will work through a basic pattern, the dishcloth (Figure 1), explaining each block and how it fits together using descriptions and photographs. Note that to make the individual blocks more clear, many photos will show multiple double pointed needles. The actual work is done on one long circular needle as shown in later photos. While this may sound complicated, if you follow through, block by block, soon you'll be turning corners like a pro.

FIGURE 1 Finished Dishcloth

This dishcloth is worked with the following materials:

✧ KnitPicks Dishie (100% cotton; 190 yards per 100 gram skein)

- [Color A] Heat Wave Multi - 25850; 1 skein, uses approximately 25 yards
- [Color B] Clementine - 25403; 1 skein, uses approximately 40 yards
- [Color C] Fiesta Red - 25786; 1 skein, uses approximately 55 yards

✧ 32–40-inch US #7/4.5mm circular needle, or size needed to obtain gauge

Gauge

18 stitches and 28 rows = 4"/10 cm in stockinette stitch. Gauge is not critical in this pattern, but a different gauge will affect yardage and size of finished item.

ROUND 1 Center row, working counterclockwise (from right to left), with Color A

BLOCK 1 Center-row-setup rectangle (Figure 2).

FIGURE 2 CCW-center-row-setup rectangle

With RS facing, provisionally cast on 6 stitches onto right needle, turn. For an easy method to provisionally cast on stitches, see Chapter 3.

Row 1 (WS): P6, turn.
Rows 2, 4, 6, 8, 10 (RS): Sl1k (slip one knitwise), k5, turn.
Rows 3, 5, 7, 9, 11: Sl1p (slip one purlwise), p5, turn.
Row 12: Sl1k, k5, do not turn.

Round 1 is complete.

Round 2 will be the first time you change direction, and the first time you change color. To avoid gaps between blocks, either join yarn as you go (see page 79), or tie ends together with a loose knot that you can untie when you are ready to sew in the ends.

ROUND 2 With Colors B and C, working clockwise (from left to right). (Figure 3)

TOP TIER Color B, working first tier of round (Figure 4).
BLOCK 1 Beginning-of-round rectangle. This is the first of the special blocks that you need at the ends of each tier to turn the corner. At the beginning of each round, the first block will be cast on provisionally and attached or joined to the last block worked in the round below. The provisional stitches will be joined later with the last block of this round, completing the rectangular round (Figure 5).

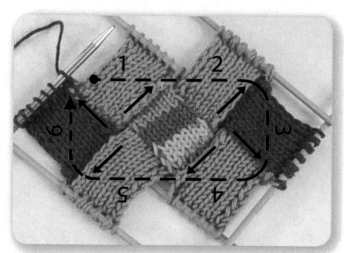

FIGURE 3 Round 2

FIGURE 4 Top Tier, First Tier of Round 2

FIGURE 5 CW Beginning-of-round Rectangle

With WS facing, provisionally cast on 6 stitches onto right (empty) needle, turn. If you wish to use another provisional cast-on method, you may find it easier to provisionally cast on onto a dpn. This way, you can work the first row (without a join), and make sure the needle is properly aligned to work the join at the end of the second row. When you are confident that the block is properly aligned, slip work from the dpn onto your working needles.

Row 1 (RS): K6, turn.

Rows 2, 4, 6, 8, 10 (WS): Sl1p, p4, p2tog (last stitch of new color with next stitch of old color), turn.

Rows 3, 5, 7, 9, 11: Sl1k, k5, turn.

Row 12: Sl1p, p5, p2tog, do not turn.

BLOCK 2 End-of-tier rectangle. This is the next of the special blocks you need at the ends of each tier to turn the corner. At the end of each tier (except the final tier which completes the round), the last block will not attach to other blocks with ssks or p2togs. (Figure 6)

FIGURE 7 Right Side Tier, Second Tier of Round 2

block just worked, you will need to pull needle in block just worked to expose extra cable. (Figures 8 & 9)

FIGURE 6 CW End-of-tier Rectangle

With WS facing, pick up 6 stitches purlwise along edge of block below; turn. See Chapter 4 for the Double Half Stitch Pickup.

Rows 1, 3, 5, 7, 9, 11 (RS): Sl1k, k5, turn.

Rows 2, 4, 6, 8, 10 (WS): Sl1p, p5, turn.

Row 12: Sl1p, p5, do not turn.

RIGHT SIDE TIER Color C, second tier of round, turning your first corner. (Figure 7)

BLOCK 3 Beginning- and end-of-tier rectangle. This is a combination of two of the special blocks you need at the ends of each tier to turn the corner. In order to work a beginning-of-tier block directly onto the end-of-tier

FIGURE 8 CW Beginning-of-tier Rectangle, Stitch Pickup

FIGURE 9 CW Beginning- and end-of-tier Rectangle

Because there is only one block on this tier, after you pick up stitches for a beginning-of-tier rectangle, you will work the remainder as an end-of-tier rectangle. With new color C and WS facing, pick up 6 stitches purlwise along edge of block just worked; turn.

Rows 1, 3, 5, 7, 9, 11 (RS): Sl1k, k5, turn.
Rows 2, 4, 6, 8, 10 (WS): Sl1p, p5, turn.
Row 12: Sl1p, p5, do not turn.

BOTTOM TIER Color B, third tier of round. The third tier will usually be similar to the first tier, except the first block will be a beginning-of-tier rectangle, not a beginning-of-round rectangle. In the Round 2 only, the provisional stitches from Round 1 will be joined to the blocks being worked, so before working the bottom tier, these stitches must be on your needle and properly mounted. (Figure 10)

FIGURE 11 CW Beginning-of-tier Rectangle

BLOCK 5 End-of-tier rectangle (same as block 2 earlier in round 2).

LEFT SIDE TIER Color C, fourth (final) tier of round. The fourth tier will usually be similar to the second tier, except the last block will be an end-of-round rectangle, not an end-of-tier rectangle. For this final block, the provisional stitches from the first block of this round will be joined to this block being worked, so these stitches must be on your needle and properly mounted. (Figure 12)

FIGURE 10 Bottom Tier, Third Tier of Round 2

BLOCK 4 Beginning-of-tier rectangle. This is another of the special blocks you need at the ends of each tier to turn the corner. In order to work a beginning-of-tier rectangle directly onto the end-of-tier rectangle just worked, you will need to pull needle in block just worked to expose extra cable. (Figure 11)

Pull needle in block just worked to expose extra cable. With new color B and WS facing, pick up 6 stitches purlwise along edge of block just worked; turn.

Rows 1, 3, 5, 7, 9, 11 (RS): Sl1k, k5, turn.
Rows 2, 4, 6, 8, 10 (WS): Sl1p, p5, p2tog, turn.
Row 12: Sl1p, p5, p2tog, do not turn.

FIGURE 12 Left Side Tier, Fourth Tier of Round 2

BLOCK 6 Beginning-of-tier and end-of-round combined rectangle. This is another combination of the special blocks you need at the ends of each tier to turn the corner. After mounting provisional stitches from first block, this is worked as a beginning-of-tier rectangle.

Pull needle in block just worked to expose extra cable. With new color C and WS facing, pick up 6 stitches purlwise along edge of block just worked; turn.

Rows 1, 3, 5, 7, 9, 11 (RS): Sl1k, k5, turn.
Rows 2, 4, 6, 8, 10 (WS): Sl1p, p4, p2tog, turn.
Row 12: Sl1p, p4, p2tog, do not turn.

Round 2 is complete

ROUND 3 With Colors A and C, working counter-clockwise. At the beginning of this round, you will change the direction of your work, but first block will still be cast on provisionally and attached or joined to the last block from the round below. All of the same special blocks are needed at the corners, they just go the other way. This change in direction also means that you will work the tiers in the following order; left side tier, bottom tier, right side tier, top tier. Each tier will also get one block wider. (Figure 13)

FIGURE 13 Round 3

LEFT SIDE TIER Color A, working first tier of round. (Figure 14)

FIGURE 14 Left Side Tier, First Tier of Round 3

BLOCK 1 Beginning-of-round rectangle. (Figure 15)

FIGURE 15 CCW Beginning-of-round Rectangle

With RS facing, provisionally cast on 6 stitches onto right (empty) needle, turn.

Row 1 (WS): P6, turn.
Rows 2, 4, 6, 8, 10 (RS): Sl1k, k4, ssk last stitch of new color with next stitch of old color, turn.
Rows 3, 5, 7, 9, 11: Sl1p, p5, turn.
Row 12: Sl1p, k4, ssk last stitch of new color with next stitch of old color, do not turn.

BLOCK 2 End-of-tier rectangle. (Figure 16)

FIGURE 16 15 CCW End-of-tier Rectangle

With RS facing, pick up 6 stitches knitwise along edge of block below; turn.

Rows 1, 3, 5, 7, 9, 11 (WS): Sl1p, p5, turn.
Rows 2, 4, 6, 8, 10 (RS): Sl1k, k5, turn.
Row 12: Sl1k, k5, do not turn.

BOTTOM TIER Color C, second tier of round. (Figure 17)

FIGURE 17 Bottom Tier, Second Tier of Round 3

BLOCK 3 Beginning-of-tier rectangle. (Figure 18)

FIGURE 18 CCW Beginning-of-tier Rectangle

Pull needle in block just worked to expose extra cable. With new color C and RS facing, pick up 6 stitches knitwise along edge of block just worked; turn.

Rows 1, 3, 5, 7, 9, 11 (WS): Sl1p, p5, turn.
Rows 2, 4, 6, 8, 10 (RS): Sl1k, k4, ssk, turn.
Row 12: Sl1k, k4, ssk, do not turn.

BLOCK 4 Middle-of-tier rectangle. (Figure 19)

FIGURE 19 CCW Middle-of-tier Rectangle

With RS facing, pick up 6 stitches knitwise, turn.

Rows 1, 3, 5, 7, 9, 11 (WS): Sl1p, p5, turn.
Rows 2, 4, 6, 8, 10 (RS): Sl1k, k4, ssk, turn.
Row 12: Sl1k, k4, ssk, do not turn.

BLOCK 5 End-of-tier rectangle (same as block 2 earlier in round 3).

RIGHT SIDE TIER Color A, third tier of round. (Figure 20)

FIGURE 20 Right Side Tier, Third Tier of Round 3

BLOCK 6 Beginning-of-tier rectangle (same as block 3 earlier in round 3).
BLOCK 7 End-of-tier rectangle (same as block 2 earlier in round 3).

TOP TIER Color C, fourth (final) tier of round. (Figure 21)

FIGURE 21 Top Tier, Fourth Tier of Round 3

FIGURE 22 Round 4

BLOCK 8 Beginning-of-tier rectangle (same as block 3 earlier in round 3).
BLOCK 9 Middle-of-tier rectangle (same as block 4 earlier in round 3).
BLOCK 10 End-of-round rectangle (after mounting provisional stitches, this is worked as a middle-of-tier rectangle).

With RS facing, pick up 6 stitches knitwise along edge of block below; turn.

Rows 1, 3, 5, 7, 9, 11 (WS): Sl1p, p5, turn.
Rows 2, 4, 6, 8, 10 (WS): Sl1k, k4, ssk, turn.
Row 12: Sl1k, k4, ssk, do not turn.

Round 3 is complete.

With three rounds worked, the pattern is established. Rounds will continue alternating between counterclockwise and clockwise rounds, with one additional middle-of-tier rectangle added to each tier each round. In Round 4, you will work your first clockwise middle-of-tier rectangle.

ROUND 4 With Colors A and B, working clockwise. (Figure 22)

TOP TIER Color A, working first tier of round.
BLOCK 1 Beginning-of-round rectangle (same as round 2, block 1).
BLOCKS 2–3 Middle-of-tier rectangles. (Figure 23)

With WS facing, pick up 6 stitches purlwise along edge of block below; turn.

Rows 1, 3, 5, 7, 9, 11 (RS): Sl1k, k5, turn.
Rows 2, 4, 6, 8, 10 (WS): Sl1p, p4, p2tog (last stitch of new color with next stitch of old color), turn.
Row 12: Sl1p, p5, p2tog, do not turn.

FIGURE 23 CCW Middle-of-tier Rectangle

BLOCK 4 End-of-tier rectangle (same as round 2, block 2).

RIGHT SIDE TIER Color B, second tier of round.
BLOCK 5 Beginning-of-tier rectangle (same as round 2, block 4).
BLOCK 6 Middle-of-tier rectangle (same as block 2 earlier in round 4).
BLOCK 7 End-of-tier rectangle (same as round 2, block 2).

BOTTOM TIER Color A, third tier of round.
BLOCK 8 Beginning-of-tier rectangle (same as round 2, block 4).
BLOCKS 9–10 Middle-of-tier rectangles (same as block 2 earlier in round 4).
BLOCK 11 End-of-tier rectangle (same as round 2, block 2).

LEFT SIDE TIER Color B, fourth (final) tier of round.
BLOCK 12 Beginning-of-tier rectangle (same as round 2, block 4).
BLOCK 13 Middle-of-tier rectangle (same as block 2 earlier in round 4).

BLOCK 14 End-of-round rectangle (after mounting provisional stitches, this is worked as a middle-of-tier rectangle).

With WS facing, pick up 6 stitches purlwise along edge of block below; turn.

Rows 1, 3, 5, 7, 9, 11 (RS): Sl1k, k5, turn.
Rows 2, 4, 6, 8, 10 (WS): Sl1p, p4, p2tog, turn.
Row 12: Sl1p, p4, p2tog, do not turn.

Round 4 is complete.

ROUND 5 With Colors C and B, working counterclockwise. In Round 5, you will bind off the side tiers, working the top and bottom tiers as usual. (Figure 24)

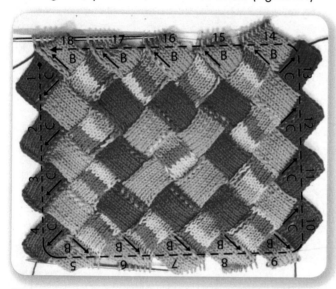

FIGURE 24 Round 5

LEFT SIDE TIER Color C, working first tier of round.
BLOCK 1 Beginning-of-round rectangle (same as round 3, block 1) binding off final row.
BLOCKS 2–3 Middle-of-tier rectangles (same as round 3, block 4), binding off final row.
BLOCK 4 End-of-tier rectangle (same as round 3, block 2), binding off final row.

BOTTOM TIER Color B, second tier of round.
BLOCK 5 Beginning-of-tier rectangle (same as round 3, block 3).
BLOCKS 6–8 Middle-of-tier rectangles (same as round 3, block 4).
BLOCK 9 End-of-tier rectangle (same as round 3, block 2).

RIGHT SIDE TIER Color C, third tier of round.
BLOCK 10 Beginning-of-tier rectangle (same as round 3, block 3), binding off final row.

BLOCKS 11–12 Middle-of-tier rectangles (same as round 3, block 4), binding off final row.
BLOCK 13 End-of-tier rectangle (same as round 3, block 2), binding off final row.

TOP TIER Color B, fourth (final) tier of round.
BLOCK 14 Beginning-of-tier rectangle (same as round 3, block 3).
BLOCKS 15–17 Middle-of-tier rectangles (same as round 3, block 4).
BLOCK 18 End-of-round rectangle (same as round 3, block 10).

Round 5 is complete.

ROUND 6 With Color C, working clockwise. On this final round, you will be working only the top and bottom tiers while binding off. (Figure 25)

FIGURE 25 Round 6

TOP TIER Color C, working first tier of round.
BLOCK 1 Cast-on rectangle, binding off final row. (Figure 26)

With WS facing, cast on 6 stitches onto right needle, turn.

Rows 1, 3, 5, 7, 9, 11 (RS): Sl1k, k5, turn.
Rows 2, 4, 6, 8, 10 (WS): Sl1p, p4, p2tog (last stitch of new color with next stitch of old color), turn.
Row 12: Sl1p, p5, p2tog, do not turn.

BLOCKS 2–5 Middle-of-tier rectangles (same as round 4, block 2), binding off final rows.
BLOCK 6 End-of-tier rectangle (same as round 2, block 2), binding off final row.

FIGURE 26 *CW Cast-on Rectangle with Bind-off*

BOTTOM TIER Color C, second tier of round.

BLOCK 7 Cast-on rectangle, binding off final row, (same as block 1, earlier in round 6).

BLOCKS 8–11 Middle-of-tier rectangles (same as round 4, block 2), binding off final rows.

BLOCK 12 End-of-tier rectangle (same as round 2, block 2), binding off final row.

Round 6 is complete. And, except for sewing in ends, so is your dishcloth.

Now that you have finished, let's look at some things that will remain consistent in other patterns. While the directions will always tell you what to do, it helps if you start to feel the rhythm too.

Stitches are picked up or cast on working in towards the center of the rectangle. The first row of a block is worked from the middle out, and the second row is worked back towards the center. If you are attaching the current block to a previous block, that will happen on the even rows.

Entrelac rectangles generally have double the number of rows as the stitches cast on, so for the 6 stitch blocks,

you work 12 rows. On blocks where you are attaching to a previous block, you may not need to count. As you work a ssk or a p2tog with the last stitch to join, you are done.

Blocks on the outside edges will be bound off in two subsequent rounds.

Now let's look at some of the things that may change; the number of stitches across each block, the number of blocks in the center row, the project shape and blocks with special shapes, and the pattern used in each block.

The patterns in this book use blocks that range from 4 to 9 stitches wide.

The rectangular patterns in this book have first rounds ranging from one block to twenty-nine blocks, but the concept is the same. To keep things simple, all the patterns, except the folk mittens, begin with entrelac blocks working counterclockwise (from right to left).

Some of the patterns are not flat rectangles, and will require additional blocks. The shawl is half a rectangle with only one corner. Instead of provisional stitches at the beginning of rounds, the blocks begin with a cast-on edge. This makes it an ideal first mitered entrelac project. The poncho and sweater have finished edges that are cast on at the beginning as well.

Most of the blocks used in this book are stockinette, but a few of the patterns feature ribbed blocks; the triangular shawl, the folk trio, the trivet, and the cape. When you are ready to work a ribbed pattern, this book has a special section on ribbed blocks.

So, how do you take all of your new skills and information, and apply it to other patterns? First, all of the standard blocks in this chapter are put together in two reference charts, one for counterclockwise, and one for clockwise. In the next chapter, Reading the Patterns, a legend will demonstrate how these blocks are shown in diagrams. Also in that chapter, you will learn how to use these tools for all of the patterns in this book.

CHART A

Counterclockwise rectangles (working from right to left, with left-slanting rectangles)

Center-row-setup rectangle	With RS facing, provisionally cast on 4 (5, 6, 7, 8, 9) stitches onto right needle, turn. **Row 1 (WS):** Purl all, turn. **Even rows (RS):** Sl1k, knit to end, turn. **Odd rows (after row 1):** Sl1p, purl to end, turn. Continue until 8 (10, 12, 14, 16, 18) rows have been worked. Do not turn after final row. Note: When working multiple center-row-setup rectangles, cast on only the stitches for one block at a time.	
Beginning-of-round rectangle	With RS facing, provisionally cast on 4 (5, 6, 7, 8, 9) stitches onto right (empty) needle, turn. **Row 1 (WS):** Purl all, turn. **Even rows (RS):** Sl1k, knit to next-to-last stitch, ssk (last stitch of new color with next stitch of old color), turn. **Odd rows (after row 1):** Sl1p, purl to end, turn. Continue until 8 (10, 12, 14, 16, 18) rows have been worked. Do not turn after final row.	
Cast-on rectangle	With RS facing, cast on 4 (5, 6, 7, 8, 9) stitches onto right needle, turn. **Odd rows (WS):** Sl1p, purl to end, turn. **Even rows (RS):** Sl1k, knit to next-to-last stitch, ssk (last stitch of new color with next stitch of old color), turn. Continue until 8 (10, 12, 14, 16, 18) rows have been worked. Do not turn after final row.	
Beginning-of-tier rectangle	Pull needle in block just worked to expose extra cable. With new color and RS facing, pick up 4 (5, 6, 7, 8, 9) stitches knitwise along edge of block just worked; turn. **Odd rows (WS):** Sl1p, purl to end, turn. **Even rows (RS):** Sl1k, knit to next-to-last stitch, ssk (last stitch of new color with next stitch of old color), turn. Continue until 8 (10, 12, 14, 16, 18) rows have been worked. Do not turn after final row.	
Middle-of-tier rectangle	With RS facing, pick up 4 (5, 6, 7, 8, 9) stitches knitwise, turn. **Odd rows (WS):** Sl1p, purl to end, turn. **Even rows (RS):** Sl1k, knit to next-to-last stitch, ssk (last stitch of new color with next stitch of old color), turn. Continue until 8 (10, 12, 14, 16, 18) rows have been worked. Do not turn after final row.	
End-of-tier rectangle	With RS facing, pick up 4 (5, 6, 7, 8, 9) stitches knitwise along edge of block below; turn. **Odd rows (WS):** Sl1p, purl to end, turn. **Even rows (RS):** Sl1k, knit to end, turn. Continue until 8 (10, 12, 14, 16, 18) rows have been worked. Do not turn after final row.	
End-of-round rectangle	Before completing the round with this final rectangle, the provisional stitches from the initial, beginning-of-round rectangle will need to be mounted, or remounted onto the opposite needle, and then worked as a middle-of-tier rectangle.	
Bind-off	Pick up stitches and work rectangle as specified to last row. Work last row as specified AND loosely bind off all stitches. Last stitch should be bound off over first picked-up stitch from next block. If last rectangle, pull yarn through last bind-off.	
Combining Beginning and Ending rectangles	If a tier contains only one block, you will combine two of the special blocks needed at the ends of each tier to turn the corner. Pick up or cast on stitches as you would for the beginning-of-round/tier rectangle or cast-on rectangle, and work rectangle as you would for end-of-round/tier rectangle.	
Ribbed rectangles	For ribbed rectangles with an odd number of stitches, the first and last stitches in each row remain as specified, beginning with a k1 on RS, and a p1 on WS. For ribbed, CCW rectangles with an even number of stitches, all rows begin with a p1.	

CHART B

Clockwise rectangles (working from left to right, with right-slanting rectangles)

Center-row-setup rectangle	With WS facing, provisionally cast on 4 (5, 6, 7, 8, 9) stitches onto right needle, turn. **Row 1 (RS):** Knit all, turn. **Even rows (WS):** Sl1p, purl to end, turn. **Odd rows (after row 1):** Sl1k, knit to end, turn. Continue until 8 (10, 12, 14, 16, 18) rows have been worked. Do not turn after final row.	
Beginning-of-round rectangle	With WS facing, provisionally cast on 4 (5, 6, 7, 8, 9) stitches onto right (empty) needle, turn. **Row 1 (RS):** Knit all, turn. **Even rows (WS):** Sl1p, purl to next-to-last stitch, p2tog (last stitch of new color with next stitch of old color), turn. **Odd rows (after row 1):** Sl1k, knit to end, turn. Continue until 8 (10, 12, 14, 16, 18) rows have been worked. Do not turn after final row.	
Cast-on rectangle	With WS facing, cast on 4 (5, 6, 7, 8, 9) stitches onto right needle, turn. To cast on knitting backwards (so your CW cast-on matches the appearance of CCW cast-on), see Casting On, page 79. **Odd rows (RS):** Sl1k, knit to end, turn. **Even rows (WS):** Sl1p, purl to next-to-last stitch, p2tog (last stitch of new color with next stitch of old color), turn. Continue until 8 (10, 12, 14, 16, 18) rows have been worked. Do not turn after final row.	
Beginning-of-tier rectangle	Pull needle in block just worked to expose extra cable. With new color and WS facing, pick up 4 (5, 6, 7, 8, 9) stitches purlwise along edge of block just worked; turn. **Odd rows (RS):** Sl1k, knit to end, turn. **Even rows (WS):** Sl1p, purl to next-to-last stitch, p2tog (last stitch of new color with next stitch of old color), turn. Continue until 8 (10, 12, 14, 16, 18) rows have been worked. Do not turn after final row.	
Middle-of-tier rectangle	With WS facing, pick up 4 (5, 6, 7, 8, 9) stitches purlwise along edge of block below; turn. **Odd rows (RS):** Sl1k, knit to end, turn. **Even rows (WS):** Sl1p, purl to next-to-last stitch, p2tog (last stitch of new color with next stitch of old color), turn. Continue until 8 (10, 12, 14, 16, 18) rows have been worked. Do not turn after final row.	
End-of-tier rectangle	With WS facing, pick up 4 (5, 6, 7, 8, 9) stitches purlwise along edge of block below; turn. **Odd rows (RS):** Sl1k, knit to end, turn. **Even rows (WS):** Sl1p, purl to end, turn. Continue until 8 (10, 12, 14, 16, 18) rows have been worked. Do not turn after final row.	
End-of-round rectangle	Before completing the round with this final rectangle, the provisional stitches from the initial, beginning-of-round rectangle will need to be mounted, or remounted onto the opposite needle, and then worked as a middle-of-tier rectangle.	
Bind-off	Pick up stitches and work rectangle as specified to last row. Work last row as specified AND loosely bind off all stitches. Last stitch should be bound off over first picked-up stitch from next block. If last rectangle, pull last stitch through last bind-off.	
Combining Beginning and Ending rectangles	If a tier contains only one block, you will combine two of the special blocks needed at the ends of each tier to turn the corner. Pick up or cast on stitches as you would for the beginning-of-round/tier rectangle or cast-on rectangle, and work rectangle as you would for end-of-round/tier rectangle.	
Ribbed rectangles	For ribbed rectangles with an odd number of stitches, the first and last stitches in each row remain as specified, beginning with a k1 on RS, and a p1 on WS. For ribbed, CW rectangles with an even number of stitches, all rows begin with a k1.	

2 READING THE PATTERNS

Now you understand the concept of turning corners in entrelac, and have followed one project through, block-by-block, learning how to work each individual block. How do you take all of those new skills and apply them to other patterns? Your most important tool will be Charts A & B, which summarize the standard blocks working clockwise and counterclockwise. You may find it helpful to place a marker on whichever chart is being used for the current round as you will be switching every round. In the patterns, you will be following diagrams, rather than pictures. Don't worry, in this chapter, we will show the pictures from the Getting Started chapter with the diagrams from the Dishcloth Pattern so you can see the transition. Your second tool will be the legend to help you read the diagrams. (Figure 1)

So now, let's work through reading the pattern.

After a picture, a title, and a description of the project, all of the information you need before starting; sizes, yarn, needles, etc. will be in a box on the right side of the page:

Finished Measurements
11" x 11"

Materials
✧ Lily Sugar'n Cream Ombres & Prints (100% cotton; 95 yards per 57 gram skein)
- [Color A] Summer Splash #1211; 1 skein, uses approximately 25 yards

✧ Lily Sugar'n Cream Solids & Denim (100% cotton; 200 yards per 115 gram skein)
- [Color B] Hot Green #18712; 1 skein, uses approximately 40 yards
- [Color C] Mod Blue#18111; 1 skein, uses approximately 55 yards

---

LEGEND for DIAGRAMS

——————	side of entrelac block
▬▬▬▬▬	side of entrelac block at corner
▬▬▬▬▬	outside edge of finished object
⟵	direction entrelac block is worked
– – –	round being worked
– – ●	beginning of round dot
◀ – -	end of round arrow
A	color letter for entrelac block
1	block number in entrelac round
	example; entrelac block, color A worked right to left (counter clockwise), beginning dot and 1 indicate first block of round
⬭	buttonhole
▭	knitting needle/cable
⅃	scrap yarn with provisional cast-on
Ⓓ	block location
—ᐯ—	break line - work does not end, but is not shown

FIGURE 1 Legend

✧ 32-40-inch US #7/4.5mm circular needle, or size needed to obtain gauge

Gauge

18 stitches and 28 rows = 4"/10 cm in stockinette stitch. Gauge is not critical in this pattern, but a different gauge will affect yardage and size of finished item.

On the left of the page are the instructions for beginning your work. Have you noticed that Charts A & B give instruction for blocks of different sizes and pattern, stockinette or ribbed? The first thing you need to know is how many stitches each block is across and what pattern to use, so that is the first information you get:

The napkin/dishcloth is worked in stockinette, with 6 stitch blocks. Chart A and Chart B refer to the mitered entrelac technique charts on pages 10 and 11.

Towards the beginning of the pattern, you will get an overall diagram of your project which will look similar to the photo at the beginning of the Getting Started chapter: (Figures 2 & 3)

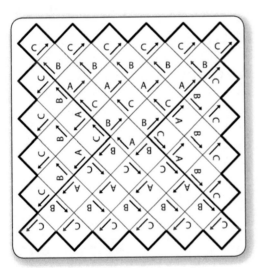

FIGURE 2 Napkin Diagram

FIGURE 3 Napkin Photo

Instructions for the rounds will look almost identical to the Getting Started chapter except they now tell you which chart, Chart A on page 10 or Chart B on page 11, to follow. The diagram of round 1 will replace the photo of the round.

ROUND 1 Center row, working counterclockwise, with Color A, follow Chart A on page 10. (Figures 4 & 5)

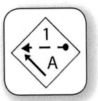

FIGURE 4
Round 1 Diagram

FIGURE 5 Round 1 Photo

Each block will specify which type of block to work, but not give row-by-row instructions or reference other blocks; that information is in Chart A on page 10 (or Chart B on page 11 for even rounds).

BLOCK 1 Center-row-setup rectangle.

Round 1 is complete.

ROUND 2 With Colors B and C, working clockwise, follow Chart B on page 11.

Round 2 is the first round to work counterclockwise, and to have all four tiers to work all the way around, so there will be a diagram. The round 2 diagram will replace all photos of the round, including individual tiers. (Figures 6 & 7)

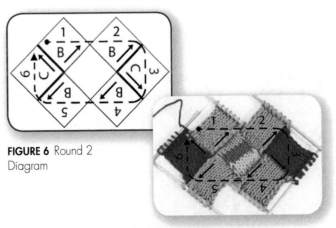

FIGURE 6 Round 2
Diagram

FIGURE 7 Round 2 Photo

TOP TIER, COLOR B
BLOCK 1 Beginning-of-round rectangle.
BLOCK 2 End-of-tier rectangle.

RIGHT SIDE TIER, COLOR C
BLOCK 3 Beginning- and end-of-tier rectangle.

BOTTOM TIER, COLOR B
BLOCK 4 Beginning-of-tier rectangle.
BLOCK 5 End-of-tier rectangle. Note that for this block, you will be picking up stitches from the bottom to the top of the entrelac block below; not top to bottom as normal. This note is important if you are using my method of picking up stitches in the next chapter, so don't worry about it now.

LEFT SIDE TIER, COLOR C
BLOCK 6 Beginning-of-tier and end-of-round combined rectangle.

Round 2 is complete.

ROUND 3 With Colors A and C, working counterclockwise, follow Chart A on page 10.

Round 3 is the first round to work all four tiers clockwise, so there will be a diagram. As with round 2, the diagram replaces all photos of the round, including individual tiers. (Figures 8 & 9)

LEFT SIDE TIER, COLOR A
BLOCK 1 Beginning-of-round rectangle.
BLOCK 2 End-of-tier rectangle.

BOTTOM TIER, COLOR C
BLOCK 3 Beginning-of-tier rectangle.
BLOCK 4 Middle-of-tier rectangle.
BLOCK 5 End-of-tier rectangle.

RIGHT SIDE TIER, COLOR A
BLOCK 6 Beginning-of-tier rectangle.
BLOCK 7 End-of-tier rectangle.

TOP TIER, COLOR C
BLOCK 8 Beginning-of-tier rectangle.
BLOCK 9 Middle-of-tier rectangle.
BLOCK 10 End-of-round rectangle.

Round 3 is complete.

Congratulations; there are no more notes needed to work Rounds 4–6. Have you noticed how the diagrams guide you through, step-by-step? You may choose to check off each block on the diagram and/or pattern as it's worked. If not, and you lose your place, just count the blocks you've already worked to find your place. You are ready to follow the patterns, but before you begin, I recommend reading the following chapters on the provisional cast-on, picking up stitches, and, if appropriate, working ribbed blocks.

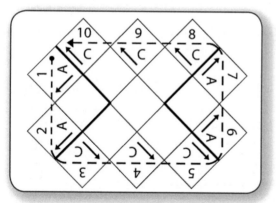

FIGURE 8 Round 3 Diagram

FIGURE 9 Round 3 Photo

3 PROVISIONAL CAST-ON

Some knitters are intimidated by the provisional cast-on, and if you are absolutely certain that this is not a knitting skill for you, you can still work the triangular shawl. However, please read a little more before you decide. Not only will the provisional cast-on allow you to work all the other patterns utilizing the new, fun technique in this book, it can open many other possibilities as well. The patterns in this book are also the easiest and lowest risk way to learn and use the provisional cast-on for several reasons.

1. You only need to provisionally cast on 4 to 9 stitches at a time, depending on your block size.

2. You can easily provisionally cast on these few stitches exactly where you need them on the cable, so you don't have to pick them up later.

3. Most importantly, while most provisional cast-ons are found somewhere highly visible like the middle of your work, or where you pick up a border, all of your stitches that were provisionally cast on will be hidden behind another stitch in an ssk or p2tog. No one will even see them!

I hope I've convinced you to try a provisional cast-on. Even if you already have a method of provisionally casting on that you generally use, this one is worth a look. Provisional cast-ons are seen many places, using scrap yarn or a cable. The basic technique begins with placing a slip knot on your needle. You hold your yarn much like a long tail cast-on with the working yarn on top, and the cable or scrap yarn on the bottom. You then pick up stitches onto your needle alternating over the cable/scrap yarn and under, resulting in working stitches on the needle, and provisional stitches for later use on the

cable/scrap yarn. Many circular shawls begin similarly, with the circle cast-on, where the stitches are picked up over and under your slip-knot loop. Here, the provisional stitches are never worked, but remain permanently on their original loop. Cat Bordhi uses a very similar technique in her moebius cast-on, but the needle is first coiled in such a way that the original working stitches, followed by the provisional stitches are all worked in every round, resulting in an infinite loop. If you have used any of these cast-ons, this one is easier. Even if you haven't, give it a try; remember, it won't even show!

Let's work through a basic rectangular pattern, the kitchen towel/placemat, beginning with round 1, the center row, worked counterclockwise. You won't be using a separate cable/scrap yarn, a center loop, or a coiled needle. Instead, with the working needle on the right, pointing left, fold your cable several inches past the needle, bringing the rest of the cable back under and past the working needle. The rest of the cable and the other needle will dangle below to the left. Place a slip knot on the working needle and slide it around on the cable until it is under your needle. Reaching over the cable, pick up one stitch on your needle. When worked after the stitches picked up under the cable, this will also create one provisional stitch on your cable. (Figures 1 & 2)

Now, reach under the cable, picking up one more stitch on your needle, which also creates a provisional stitch on your cable. (Figures 3 & 4)

Alternating over and under the cable, pick up the desired number of stitches for the first block only. Note that you only count the stitches on the working needle, not on the cable below. Do not count the slip knot; it will not be worked and will be slipped off the needle later. (Figures 5 & 6)

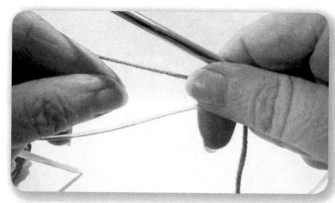

FIGURE 1 Provisional Cast-on Setup

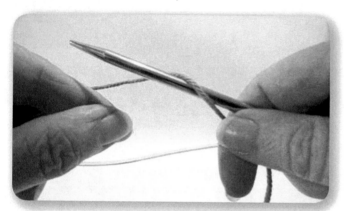

FIGURE 2 Stitch Over Cable

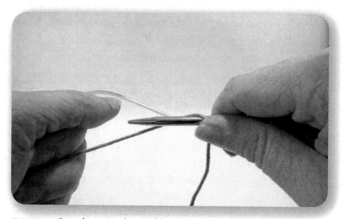

FIGURE 3 Reaching Under Cable

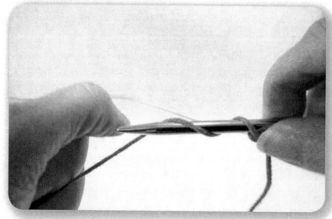

FIGURE 4 Stitch Under Cable

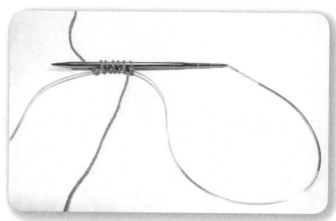

FIGURE 5 Block 1 stitches

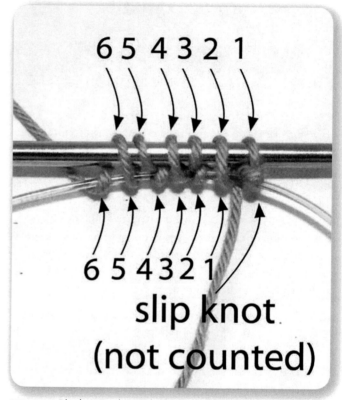

FIGURE 6 Block 1 Stitches, Close Up

After working a center-row-setup rectangle counter-clockwise, your project will look like this: (Figure 7)

To provisionally cast on the stitches for the second block, fold the first block in half, bringing the lower cable directly under the working needle, and cast stitches on as for first block, but with no slip knot. Begin by reaching over the needle, so you don't create an extra provisional stitch on the cable. (Figure 8)

After completing round 1, the four center-row-setup rectangles, your project will look like this: (Figure 9)

Round 2 is worked clockwise, and the first block is a beginning-of-round rectangle which has a provisional cast-on and is found in the top tier. This provisional cast-on will be worked with the wrong side (WS) facing. The block just worked will be on the left needle, and

FIGURE 7 First Block

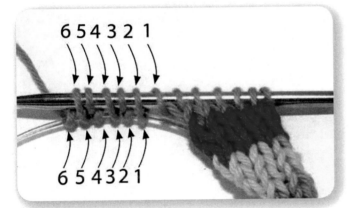

FIGURE 8 Second Block Cast On

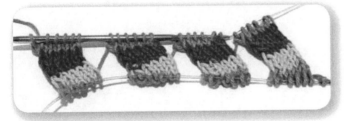

FIGURE 9 Round 1 Complete

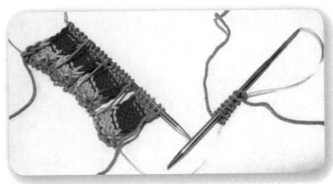

FIGURE 10 Round 2, Block 1 Cast On

FIGURE 11 Round 2, Block 1 Complete

FIGURE 12 Round 2, Bottom Tier

the right needle will be empty, with extra cable. Just as you did at the beginning of round 1, place a slip knot under the working needle and then reaching alternately over and under the cable, pick up the desired number of stitches for the block. Remember that you only count the stitches on the working needle, and do not count the slip knot. (Figure 10)

After working beginning-of-round rectangle clockwise, your project will look like this: (Figure 11)

Now, let's continue to work round 2 and see how our provisional stitches occur exactly where we need them. After completing the top tier and the right side tier, you will be ready to work the bottom tier. Except for the end-of-tier rectangle, all of the round 2, bottom tier rectangles will attach or join to the provisional stitches

from your round 1 blocks. Looking at your work, they are exactly where you need them. (Figure 12)

Before working the bottom tier, remove the slip knot. Half of these provisional stitches are mounted backwards, with the right leg (or side) of the stitch behind your needle rather than in front. Before working each bottom tier block, take a moment to slide these provisional stitches back and forth between your two needles, mounting them properly. When the bottom tier is finished, and you are ready to work the left side tier, the provisional stitches from the round 2, beginning-of-round rectangle are just where you need them, but will also need to have the slip knot dropped and be remounted before proceeding. (Figure 13)

FIGURE 13 Round 2, Left Side Tier

After working the left side tier, round 2 is complete. (Figure 14)

FIGURE 14 Round 2 Complete

Round 3 is worked counterclockwise, and the first block is a beginning-of-round rectangle which has a provisional cast-on and is found in the left tier. This provisional cast-on will be worked with the right side (RS) facing. The block just worked will be on the left needle, and the right needle will be empty, with extra cable. Just as you did at the beginning of rounds 1 and 2, place a slip knot under the working needle and then, reaching alternately over and under the cable, pick up the desired number of stitches for the block. Remember that you only count the stitches on the working needle, and do not count the slip knot. (Figure 15)

FIGURE 15 Round 3, Block 1 Cast On

After working the beginning-of-round rectangle counterclockwise, your project will look like this: (Figure 16)

The provisional stitches are pointed up and to the right, just where you will need to join them to the end-of-round rectangle at the left end of the top tier, after they are remounted, and the slip knot is dropped.

Subsequent rounds that begin with beginning-of-round rectangles will be worked in a similar way, even rounds like round 2 and odd rounds like round 3.

As your project gets larger, you may have to pull a little harder to get the extra cable you need for the provisional cast-on, and you might even need to switch to a longer needle.

FIGURE 16 Round 3, Block 1 Complete

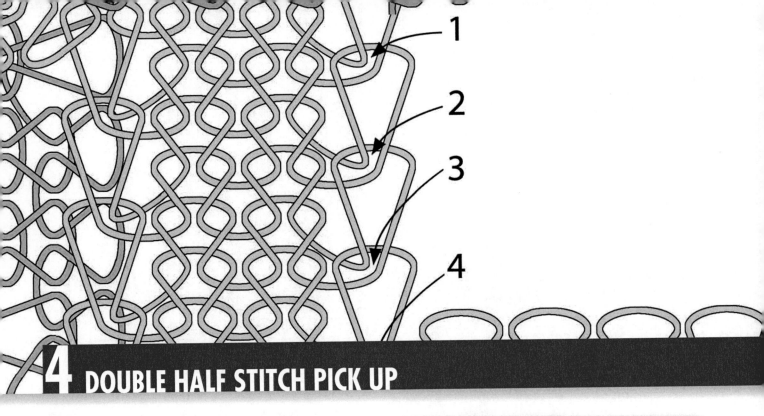

1
2
3
4

4 DOUBLE HALF STITCH PICK UP

By the time most knitters learn entrelac, they are likely very comfortable with knitting and purling and decreasing stitches, ssks and p2togs, but may not have as much experience with picking up stitches. Because you will be picking up stitches to begin most of your entrelac blocks, it is essential to become comfortable with this skill. Ideally, you want to pick up stitches in a way that doesn't hide too much of your valuable work in a bulky selvedge, and doesn't leave noticeable holes either. I also like to slip the first stitch of each row for a smoother edge and less bulk in the selvedge. There are some slight differences in these slipped-stitch selvedges. I use the French method: if the first stitch of a row would normally be knit, it is slipped knitwise; if the first stitch of a row would normally be purled, it is slipped purlwise. Let's look at two common methods for picking up stitches using a graphic that makes it easier to see what's going on.

PICKING UP BETWEEN TWO STITCHES

Picking up new stitches between the two stitches at the edge of your work has the advantage of creating a smooth edge that looks smooth on the front of your work, but let's look at the disadvantages. On the back of your work, there is a whole stitch now facing the opposite way that is fairly bulky and noticeable. Depending on the type of garment, this may or may not be important, but there's another disadvantage. You just lost a whole stitch at the edge of your block. In most knitting, one stitch at the edge doesn't represent a significant proportion of your

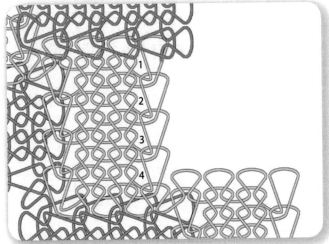

FIGURE 1 1 Picking Up Between Two Stitches

work, but entrelac is made up of many small blocks. If your block is only 5 stitches wide, one stitch represents 20% of your work hidden in your selvedge. Would you pay that kind of tax without at least looking for a better alternative? (Figure 1)

PICKING UP IN THE MIDDLE OF EDGE STITCHES

Picking up new stitches in the middle of an edge stitch has the advantage of minimizing the work lost in the selvedge, and that half stitch may be less noticeable on the back. Unfortunately, your new stitch pulls on the long leg of a stitch, and it tends to pull sideways and make gaps in your work. (Figure 2)

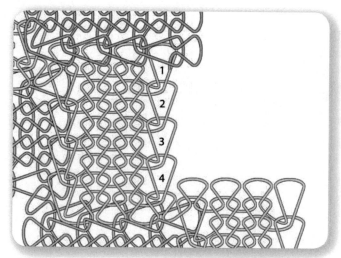

FIGURE 2 1 Picking Up in the Middle of Edge Stitches

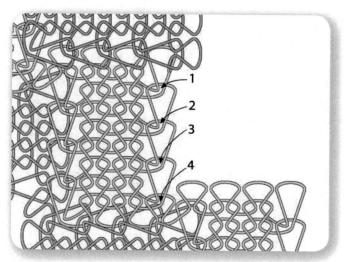

FIGURE 3 A Better Alternative

LOOKING FOR A BETTER ALTERNATIVE

So, when picking up new stitches between the two stitches at the edge, you have the advantage of pulling the new stitch through two legs of yarn at the same time, avoiding gaps. And, when picking up new stitches in the middle of the edge stitch, you have the advantage of a smaller selvedge and less work hidden. In addition to their individual disadvantages, both methods have one other disadvantage in common. With your slipped stitch selvedge, there is always one extra edge stitch, from the pickup row. That means you always have one more stitch at the edge than these first two pickup methods use. This often leads to holes at the corners where your entrelac blocks meet, no matter how gap-free they are along the pickup edge. Wouldn't it be nice to have the advantages, but not the disadvantages, of the first two methods, and use all of your selvedge stitches for beautiful corners? Let's take another look at the diagram. There is another place to pick up stitches, both in the middle of the stitch, and pulling through two legs of yarn, using all of your edge stitches.

While it may be easy to see where you want to pick up new stitches on a diagram with large gaps, let's look at how it works with real yarn. (Figure 3)

DOUBLE HALF STITCH PICKUP

There's a trick to this stitch pickup; you will use the left needle to pick up two legs of yarn, and then knit or purl the two legs together as two stitches, creating one new stitch. Before knitting or purling, you will want these two legs to appear as two uncrossed stitches, so it will matter if you pick them up from front-to-back or back-to-front. We will work through the possibilities, clockwise and counterclockwise, top-to-bottom, and bottom-to top, but you will also learn to recognize when the legs are picked up properly. Let's work through the possibilities as you

will encounter them in the patterns using the same example from the previous chapter, the kitchen towel, worked with 6-stitch rectangles.

For most of the patterns in this book, you will begin picking up stitches in Round 2. After the beginning-of-round rectangle, where the stitches are provisionally cast on, you will be working clockwise, picking up stitches from the edges of stockinette blocks oriented top-to-bottom.

In the photo below, the blocks are 6-stitch blocks, so there is one row picked up and 12 rows worked. This means that along the edge where you need to pick up stitches, there are seven stitches as shown. Stitch 1 is the leg between two blocks; for later blocks, it will be from the row you picked up from the block below. Stitches 2–7 are all double sized stitches because you slipped the first stitch of each row. The last stitch in this block, stitch 7, will have just been joined to the previous block with a p2tog, but you will still be using it (Figure 4).

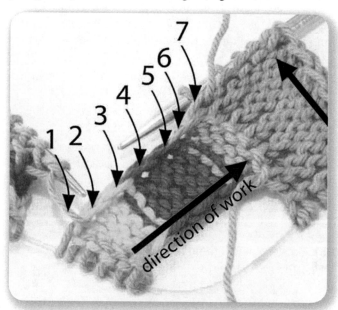

FIGURE 4 CW Legs for Stitch Pick Up

Our first stitch picked up will be picked up through the outside legs of stitches 6 and 7. Because the block from which the stitches will be picked up is oriented top-to-bottom, with purled edge stitches, the stitch 7 leg crosses behind the stitch 6 leg. This means that you will pick the legs up from the front, so they don't cross. So, with WS facing, using left needle, working from front-to-back, pick up next-to-last stitch leg, leg 6, and then pick up last stitch leg, leg 7. These will look like two stitches, mounted properly on needle. (Figure 5)

FIGURE 5 CW Legs Picked Up for First Stitch

If you had mistakenly picked up the stitches from back-to-front instead, they would look twisted together, not like two individual stitches, and it would be almost impossible to put the right needle through both stitches. (Figure 6)

FIGURE 6 Twisted "Stitches"

The WS is facing you, so you will work the two legs picked up as a p2tog. Because the stitches are mounted properly, you will work a regular p2tog.

For the second stitch pick up, still with WS facing, using left needle, and working from front-to-back, pick up next-to-last stitch leg, now leg 5, and then pick up last stitch leg, now leg 6; p2tog.

Continuing in the same manner, for the third stitch pickup, pick up next-to-last stitch leg, now leg 4, and then pick up last stitch leg, now leg 5; p2tog.

Continue in the same manner until you have picked up the correct number of stitches. Note that the last leg you use, leg 1, will be from the pick-up row from the block below, and will not be as large as the other legs. You may have to work a bit harder to pick it up. Do you notice that because blocks always have twice as many rows as stitches across, but also because you slipped the first stitch of each row, you have exactly the same number of long stitch legs as the number of stitches you will need to pick up? With the additional short leg from the pick-up row, you should always have exactly the number of legs you need, resulting in a firm pickup with no gaps. (Figures 7 & 8)

FIGURE 7 RS of Work

FIGURE 8 WS of Work

Other block orientations will have similarly beautiful results with no gaps, and small selvedges, but will be worked slightly differently.

Along the bottom tier of round 2, all of the blocks after the beginning-of-tier rectangle, are picked up from the bottom of the round 1, center-row-setup rectangle(s). This means you will still be working counterclockwise, but along this bottom edge of the stockinette blocks, the edge stitches are oriented from bottom-to-top. (Figure 9)

Because the block from which the stitches will be picked up is oriented bottom-to-top, leg 1, the smaller leg from the pick-up row, is now part of the stitch that was just worked in the p2tog with the previous block, and your first stitch picked up will be worked with legs 1 and 2. Also, the stitch 1 leg crosses on top of the stitch 2 leg. This means that you will pick the legs up from behind, so they don't cross. So, with WS facing, using left needle, working from back-to-front, pick up next-to-last

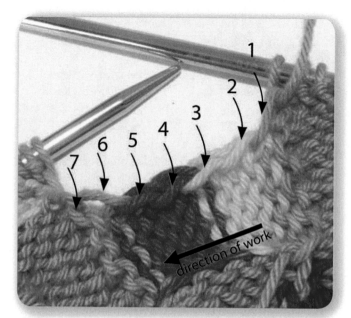

FIGURE 9 CW Legs (bottom-to-top) for Stitch Pick Up

stitch leg, leg 2, and then pick up last stitch leg, leg 1. These will look like two stitches, mounted backwards on needle (Figure 10).

FIGURE 10 CW (bottom-to-top) Legs Picked Up for First Stitch

The WS is facing you, so you will work the two legs picked up as a p2tog. Because the stitches are mounted backwards, you will work the p2tog tbl (through the back loop). Continue in the same manner until you have picked up the correct number of stitches. Notice that when you are working between two center-row-setup rectangles, leg 7 is in an odd location. By the time this final stitch leg was pulled across to pick up provisional stitches for the next block, and then pulled again when it was worked in the block above in the top tier, it does not look like the other legs. Depending on how you

worked your provisional cast-on, and how you picked up stitches, yours may look different in another way. I find that putting the left needle through this leg 7, and then through leg 6, from front-to-back and then working a regular p2tog gives the best result for this final stitch. For the final (or only) center-row-setup rectangle, leg 7 will actually be the yarn tail. Just put your left needle under it, back-to-front, and then leg 6, and work as the other stitches. After completing this bottom tier of round 2, all remaining blocks will be oriented top-to-bottom. So, clockwise stockinette blocks will be picked up from top-to-bottom rectangles for the remainder of round 2 and for other even rounds.

In round 3 and subsequent odd rounds, you will be working counterclockwise, and picking up stitches from the edges of stockinette blocks oriented top-to-bottom (Figure 11).

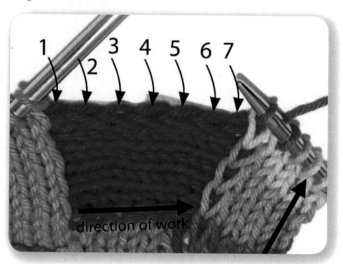

FIGURE 11 CCW Legs for Stitch Pick Up

As for other top-to-bottom blocks, the first stitch picked up will be picked up through the outside legs of stitches 6 and 7. These edge stitches have a tendency to curl to the back, and you may need to reach behind a bit to get the outside leg. Looking at Figure 12, the edge stitches are knit, so the stitch 7 leg crosses on top of the stitch 6 leg. This means that you will pick the legs up from the back, so they don't cross. So, with RS facing, using left needle, working from back-to-front, pick up next-to-last stitch leg, leg 6, and then pick up last stitch leg, leg 7. These will look like two stitches, mounted backwards on needle (Figure 12).

The RS is facing you, so you will work the two legs picked up as a K2tog. Because the stitches are mounted backwards, you will work the K2tog tbl (through the back loop). Continue in the same manner until you have picked up the correct number of stitches.

Now that you've worked through the various possibilities with the double half stitch pickup, let's look

FIGURE 12 CCW Legs Picked Up for First Stitch

at what remains consistent. You are always picking up legs with your left needle, from left-to-right. For all blocks except the few (or one) blocks picked up from the bottom edge of the center-row-setup rectangles, you are picking up from top-to-bottom. For all of your top-to-bottom rectangles, you insert your left needle into the purl side of your stitch. For stockinette, as shown, this means that when you are picking up stitches on the WS (wrong side), you are on the purled side, so your left needle is inserted from front-to-back, into the purl side of the stitch. When you are picking up stitches on the RS (right side), you are on the knit side, so your left needle

is inserted from back-to-front, (still) into the purl. Since the bottom-to-top rectangles are "upside down" from all the others, the leg crossing is reversed, so front-to-back becomes back-to-front. When in doubt, let your needle guide you. If the leg "stitches" are difficult to pick up, appear twisted on the needle, and are even more difficult to work, try inserting your needle from the other direction. Finally, no matter how you picked up your two leg "stitches," if the stitches are properly mounted, you work a regular k2tog or p2tog. If they are mounted backwards, work your k2tog or p2tog tbl (through the back loop). Whether you are working k2togs or p2togs depends only on whether you are looking at the RS (knit) or WS (purl).

A QUICK LOOK AT PICKING UP STITCHES FROM RIBBED BLOCKS

When working ribbed blocks with an odd number of stitches in each row, all edge stitches on both sides of the blocks are identical to stockinette blocks, so all of the instructions above are the same. When working ribbed blocks with an even number of stitches in each row, the stitches found toward the center of your work remain the same (so you will still be knitting to join on the front and purling to join on the back). The stitches found at the outside edge are reversed; knits are now purls and vice versa. This means that wherever you picked up stitches from front-to back and worked them regularly, you will now pick them up from back-to-front and work them through the back loop. Conversely, wherever you picked up stitches from back-to-front and worked them through the back loop, you will now pick them up from front-to-back and work them regularly. For a more complete look at working ribbed blocks, please see the next chapter.

5 WORKING RIBBED BLOCKS

Most of the blocks used in this book are stockinette, and until you are working a pattern that features ribbing (the triangular shawl, the folk trio, the trivet, or the cape) you might want to skip this chapter. The blocks that are ribbed are single stitch ribbing (k1, p1 or p1, k1). The most important stitch in an entrelac row is the stitch in even rows that attaches or joins, a p2tog for clockwise rounds, or a ssk for counterclockwise rounds. To make sure that this final stitch of the even rows lines up properly, how you work ribbed blocks is based on whether the blocks begin with an odd or even number of stitches.

When working ribbed blocks with an odd number of stitches, the first and last stitches are the same as a stockinette block with the same number of stitches; the knits or purls worked to create ribbing are all interior stitches. Take a five stitch block as an example.

For a counterclockwise, 5 stitch, stockinette, middle-of-tier rectangle the directions are:

With RS facing, pick up 5 stitches knitwise, turn.

Rows 1, 3, 5, 7, 9 (WS): Sl1p, p4, turn.
Rows 2, 4, 6, 8 (RS): Sl1k, k3, ssk, turn.
Row 10: Sl1k, k3, ssk, do not turn.
For a counterclockwise, 5 stitch, p1/k1rib, middle-of-tier rectangle the directions are:

With RS facing, pick up 5 stitches knitwise, turn. Note all stitches are still picked up knitwise.

Rows 1, 3, 5, 7, 9 (WS): Sl1p, k1, p1, k1, p1, turn.
Rows 2, 4, 6, 8 (RS): Sl1k, p1, k1, p1, ssk, turn.
Row 10: Sl1k, p1, k1, p1, ssk, do not turn.

For a clockwise, 5 stitch, stockinette, middle-of-tier rectangle the directions are:

With WS facing, pick up 5 stitches purlwise, turn.

Rows 1, 3, 5, 7, 9 (RS): Sl1k, k4, turn.
Rows 2, 4, 6, 8 (WS): Sl1p, p3, p2tog, turn.
Row 10: Sl1p, p3, p2tog, do not turn.

For a clockwise, 5 stitch, k1/p1 rib, middle-of-tier rectangle the directions are:

With WS facing, pick up 5 stitches purlwise, turn.

Rows 1, 3, 5, 7, 9 (RS): Sl1k, p1, k1, p1, k1, turn.
Rows 2, 4, 6, 8 (WS): Sl1p, k1, p1, k1, p2tog, turn.
Row 10: Sl1p, k1, p1, k1, p2tog, do not turn.

To keep things simpler, all of the ribbed blocks in this book have an odd number of stitches, except the larger size folk mittens. Unless you are making those, you might want to skip this. With an even number of stitches in a ribbed block, we will need to adjust the rows to keep the ssks or p2togs that join blocks where they need to be. That means that on even rows, we will be omitting the first stitch, leaving the joining stitch at the end where it belongs. On odd rows, we will be omitting the last stitch (which would have been the first stitch of the other side).

For a counterclockwise, 4 stitch, stockinette, middle-of-tier rectangle the directions are:

With RS facing, pick up 4 stitches knitwise, turn.

Rows 1, 3, 5, 7 (WS): Sl1p, p3, turn.
Rows 2, 4, 6 (RS): Sl1k, k2, ssk, turn.
Row 8: Sl1k, k2, ssk, do not turn.

For a counterclockwise, 4 stitch, p1/k1rib, middle-of-tier rectangle the directions are:

With RS facing, pick up 4 stitches knitwise, turn. Note all stitches are still picked up knitwise.

Rows 1, 3, 5, 7 (WS): Sl1p, k1, p1, k1, turn.
Rows 2, 4, 6 (RS): Sl1p, k1, p1, ssk, turn.
Row 8: Sl1p, k1, p1, ssk, do not turn.

Notice that for a counterclockwise, even stitch, p1/k1 rib rectangle, every row begins with a stitch slipped purlwise, followed by a knit, continuing across and ending with a knit or an ssk.

For a clockwise, 4 stitch, stockinette, middle-of-tier rectangle the directions are:

With WS facing, pick up 4 stitches purlwise, turn.

Rows 1, 3, 5, 7 (RS): Sl1k, k3, turn.
Rows 2, 4, 6 (WS): Sl1p, p2, p2tog, turn.
Row 8: Sl1p, p2, p2tog, do not turn.

For a clockwise, 5 stitch, k1/p1 rib, middle-of-tier rectangle the directions are:

With WS facing, pick up 4 stitches purlwise, turn.

Rows 1, 3, 5, 7 (RS): Sl1k, p1, k1, p1, turn.
Rows 2, 4, 6 (WS): Sl1k, p1, k1, p2tog, turn.
Row 8: Sl1k, p1, k1, p2tog, do not turn.

Notice that for a clockwise, even stitch, k1/p1 rib rectangle, every row begins with a stitch slipped knitwise, followed by a purl, continuing across and ending with a purl or a p2tog.

6 TRIANGULAR SHAWL

Finished Measurements
Wingspan: 45"
Depth: 21"

Materials

✧ Berroco Ultra Alpaca (50% alpaca, 50% wool; 215 yards per 100 gram skein)
  • [A] Black #6245; 1 skein
  • [B] Salt and Pepper #6207; 1 skein
  • [C] Light Grey #6206; 1 skein
✧ 40–47-inch US #8/5mm circular needle, or size needed to obtain gauge

Gauge
24 stitches and 32 rows = 4"/10 cm in k1, p1 ribbing. Gauge is not critical in this pattern, but a different gauge will affect yardage and size of finished item.

With only one corner to turn and no provisional cast-on, the triangular shawl is a great introduction to mitered entrelac.

With only one corner to turn and no provisional cast-on, the triangular shawl is a great introduction to mitered entrelac. You may like it so much that you want to keep going for a larger shawl, but if you do, you'll need more yarn. The shawl as shown uses up most of all three skeins (Figure 1).

The shawl is worked in k1, p1 ribbing, with 7 stitch blocks. Chart A and Chart B refer to the mitered entrelac technique charts on pages 10 and 11.

ROUND 1 Center row, working counterclockwise (from right to left), with Colors B and A, follow Chart A on page 10. (Figure 2)

LEFT SIDE TIER, COLOR B
BLOCK 1 Cast on 7 stitches, and work as end-of-tier rectangle.

RIGHT SIDE TIER, COLOR A
BLOCK 2 Beginning- and end-of-tier rectangle.

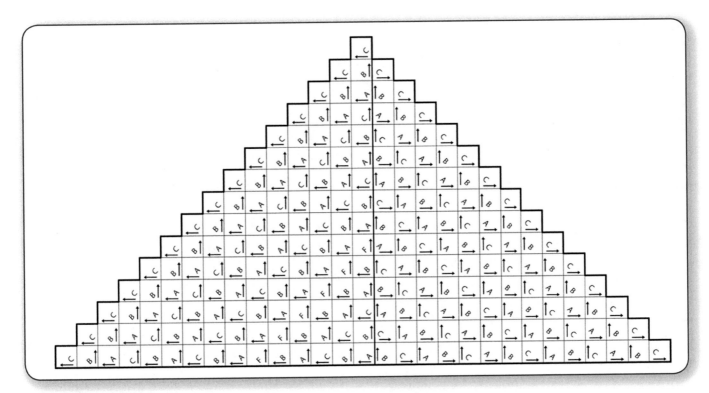

FIGURE 1 Shawl Diagram

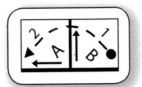

FIGURE 2 Round 1

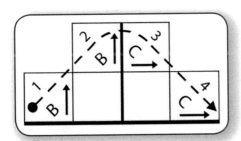

FIGURE 3 Round 2

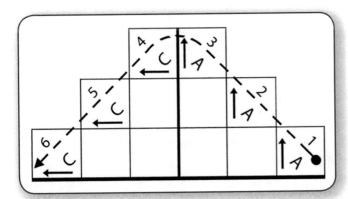

FIGURE 4 Round 3

ROUND 2 With Colors B and C, working clockwise (from left to right), follow Chart B on page 11 (Figure 3).

RIGHT SIDE TIER, COLOR B
BLOCK 1 Cast-on rectangle.
BLOCK 2 End-of-tier rectangle.

LEFT SIDE TIER, COLOR C
BLOCK 3 Beginning-of-tier rectangle.
BLOCK 4 End-of-tier rectangle. Note that for this block, you will be picking up stitches from the bottom to the top of the entrelac block below; not top to bottom as normal.

ROUND 3 With Colors A and C, working counter-clockwise, follow Chart A on page 10 (Figure 4).

LEFT SIDE TIER, COLOR A
BLOCK 1 Cast-on rectangle.
BLOCK 2 Middle-of-tier rectangle.
BLOCK 3 End-of-tier rectangle.

RIGHT SIDE TIER, COLOR C
BLOCK 4 Beginning-of-tier rectangle.
BLOCK 5 Middle-of-tier rectangle.
BLOCK 6 End-of-tier rectangle.

ROUND 4 With Colors A and B, working clockwise, follow Chart B on page 11.

RIGHT SIDE TIER, COLOR A
BLOCK 1 Cast-on rectangle.
BLOCKS 2–3 Middle-of-tier rectangles.
BLOCK 4 End-of-tier rectangle.

LEFT SIDE TIER, COLOR B
BLOCK 5 Beginning-of-tier rectangle.
BLOCKS 6–7 Middle-of-tier rectangles.
BLOCK 8 End-of-tier rectangle.

ROUND 5 With Colors C and B, working counter-clockwise, follow Chart A on page 10.

LEFT SIDE TIER, COLOR C
BLOCK 1 Cast-on rectangle.
BLOCKS 2–4 Middle-of-tier rectangles.
BLOCK 5 End-of-tier rectangle.

RIGHT SIDE TIER, COLOR B
BLOCK 6 Beginning-of-tier rectangle.
BLOCKS 7–9 Middle-of-tier rectangles.
BLOCK 10 End-of-tier rectangle.

ROUND 6 With Colors C and A, working clockwise, follow Chart B on page 11.

RIGHT SIDE TIER, COLOR C
BLOCK 1 Cast-on rectangle.
BLOCKS 2–5 Middle-of-tier rectangles.
BLOCK 6 End-of-tier rectangle.

LEFT SIDE TIER, COLOR A
BLOCK 7 Beginning-of-tier rectangle.
BLOCKS 8–11 Middle-of-tier rectangles.
BLOCK 12 End-of-tier rectangle.

ROUND 7 With Colors B and A, working counter-clockwise), follow Chart A on page 10.

LEFT SIDE TIER, COLOR B
BLOCK 1 Cast-on rectangle.
BLOCKS 2–6 Middle-of-tier rectangles.
BLOCK 7 End-of-tier rectangle.

RIGHT SIDE TIER, COLOR A
BLOCK 8 Beginning-of-tier rectangle.
BLOCKS 9–13 Middle-of-tier rectangles.
BLOCK 14 End-of-tier rectangle.

ROUND 8 With Colors B and C, working clockwise, follow Chart B on page 11.

RIGHT SIDE TIER, COLOR B
BLOCK 1 Cast-on rectangle.
BLOCKS 2–7 Middle-of-tier rectangles.
BLOCK 8 End-of-tier rectangle.

LEFT SIDE TIER, COLOR C
BLOCK 9 Beginning-of-tier rectangle.
BLOCKS 10–15 Middle-of-tier rectangles.
BLOCK 16 End-of-tier rectangle.

ROUND 9 With Colors A and C, working counter-clockwise, follow Chart A on page 10.

LEFT SIDE TIER, COLOR A
BLOCK 1 Cast-on rectangle.
BLOCKS 2–8 Middle-of-tier rectangles.
BLOCK 9 End-of-tier rectangle.

RIGHT SIDE TIER, COLOR C
BLOCK 10 Beginning-of-tier rectangle.
BLOCKS 11–17 Middle-of-tier rectangles.
BLOCK 18 End-of-tier rectangle.

ROUND 10 With Colors A and B, working clockwise, follow Chart B on page 11.

RIGHT SIDE TIER, COLOR A
BLOCK 1 Cast-on rectangle.
BLOCKS 2–9 Middle-of-tier rectangles.
BLOCK 10 End-of-tier rectangle.

LEFT SIDE TIER, COLOR B
BLOCK 11 Beginning-of-tier rectangle.
BLOCKS 12–19 Middle-of-tier rectangles.
BLOCK 20 End-of-tier rectangle.

ROUND 11 With Colors C and B, working counter-clockwise, follow Chart A on page 10.

LEFT SIDE TIER, COLOR C
BLOCK 1 Cast-on rectangle.
BLOCKS 2–10 Middle-of-tier rectangles.
BLOCK 11 End-of-tier rectangle.

RIGHT SIDE TIER, COLOR B
BLOCK 12 Beginning-of-tier rectangle.
BLOCKS 13–21 Middle-of-tier rectangles.
BLOCK 22 End-of-tier rectangle.

ROUND 12 With Colors C and A, working clockwise, follow Chart B on page 11.

RIGHT SIDE TIER, COLOR C
BLOCK 1 Cast-on rectangle.
BLOCKS 2–11 Middle-of-tier rectangles.
BLOCK 12 End-of-tier rectangle.

LEFT SIDE TIER, COLOR A
BLOCK 13 Beginning-of-tier rectangle.
BLOCKS 14–23 Middle-of-tier rectangles.
BLOCK 24 End-of-tier rectangle.

ROUND 13 With Colors B and A, working counter-clockwise, follow Chart A on page 10.

LEFT SIDE TIER, COLOR B
BLOCK 1 Cast-on rectangle.
BLOCKS 2–12 Middle-of-tier rectangles.
BLOCK 13 End-of-tier rectangle.

RIGHT SIDE TIER, COLOR A
BLOCK 14 Beginning-of-tier rectangle.
BLOCKS 15–25 Middle-of-tier rectangles.
BLOCK 26 End-of-tier rectangle.

ROUND 14 With Colors B and C, working clockwise, follow Chart B on page 11.

RIGHT SIDE TIER, COLOR B
BLOCK 1 Cast-on rectangle.
BLOCKS 2–13 Middle-of-tier rectangles.
BLOCK 14 End-of-tier rectangle.

LEFT SIDE TIER, COLOR C
BLOCK 15 Beginning-of-tier rectangle with bind-off.
BLOCKS 16–27 Middle-of-tier rectangles with bind-off.
BLOCK 28 End-of-tier rectangle with bind-off.

ROUND 15 With Color C, working counterclockwise, follow Chart A on page 10.

RIGHT SIDE TIER, COLOR C
BLOCK 1 Cast-on rectangle with bind-off.
BLOCKS 2–14 Middle-of-tier rectangle with bind-off.
BLOCK 15 End-of-tier rectangle with bind-off.

FINISHING

Sew in ends. See Appendix, Entrelac Tips, Terms and Techniques, Sewing in Ends, for tips on how to have a neatly finished edge. Wash and block.

Finished Measurements
11" x 11"

Materials
- ◇ Lily Sugar'n Cream Ombres & Prints (100% cotton; 95 yards per 57 gram skein)
  - [Color A] Summer Splash #1211; 1 skein, uses approximately 25 yards
- ◇ Lily Sugar'n Cream Solids & Denim (100% cotton; 200 yards per 115 gram skein)
  - [Color B] Hot Green #18712; 1 skein, uses approximately 40 yards
  - [Color C] Mod Blue#18111; 1 skein, uses approximately 55 yards
- ◇ 32–40-inch US #7 / 4.5mm circular needle, or size needed to obtain gauge

Gauge
18 stitches and 28 rows = 4" / 10 cm in stockinette stitch. Gauge is not critical in this pattern, but a different gauge will affect yardage and size of finished item.

7 NAPKIN/DISHCLOTH

This pattern is a perfect introduction to the mitered entrelac technique. Whether worked individually or as a set, with just a little cotton you can easily complement any kitchen décor by creating items that you'll enjoy using every day.

The napkin/dishcloth is worked in stockinette, with 6 stitch blocks. Chart A and Chart B refer to the mitered entrelac technique charts on pages 10 and 11. (Figure 1)

ROUND 1 Center row, working counterclockwise (from right to left), with Color A, follow Chart A on page 10. (Figure 2)

BLOCK 1 Center-row-setup rectangle.

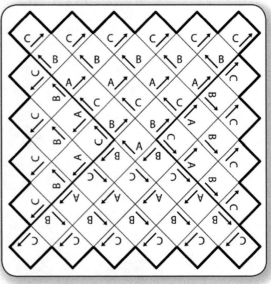

FIGURE 1 Napkin/Dishcloth Diagram

ROUND 2 With Colors B and C, working clockwise, follow Chart B on page 11. (Figure 3)

FIGURE 2 Round 1

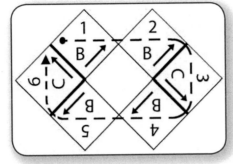

FIGURE 3 Round 2

TOP TIER, COLOR B
BLOCK 1 Beginning-of-round rectangle.
BLOCK 2 End-of-tier rectangle.

RIGHT SIDE TIER, COLOR C
BLOCK 3 Beginning- and end-of-tier rectangle.

BOTTOM TIER, COLOR B
BLOCK 4 Beginning-of-tier rectangle.
BLOCK 5 End-of-tier rectangle. Note that for this block, you will be picking up stitches from the bottom to the top of the entrelac block below; not top to bottom as normal.

LEFT SIDE TIER, COLOR C
BLOCK 6 Beginning-of-tier and end-of-round combined rectangle.

ROUND 3 With Colors A and C, working counterclockwise, follow Chart A on page 10. (Figure 4)

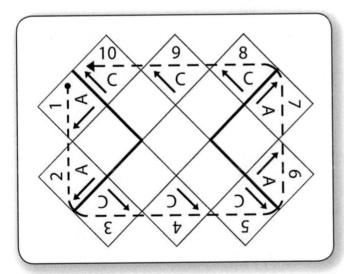

FIGURE 4 Round 3

LEFT SIDE TIER, COLOR A
BLOCK 1 Beginning-of-round rectangle.
BLOCK 2 End-of-tier rectangle.

BOTTOM TIER, COLOR C
BLOCK 3 Beginning-of-tier rectangle.
BLOCK 4 Middle-of-tier rectangle.
BLOCK 5 End-of-tier rectangle.

RIGHT SIDE TIER, COLOR A
BLOCK 6 Beginning-of-tier rectangle.
BLOCK 7 End-of-tier rectangle.

TOP TIER, COLOR C
BLOCK 8 Beginning-of-tier rectangle.
BLOCK 9 Middle-of-tier rectangle.
BLOCK 10 End-of-round rectangle.

ROUND 4 With Colors A and B, working clockwise, follow Chart B on page 11.

TOP TIER, COLOR A
BLOCK 1 Beginning-of-round rectangle.
BLOCKS 2–3 Middle-of-tier rectangles.
BLOCK 4 End-of-tier rectangle.

RIGHT SIDE TIER, COLOR B
BLOCK 5 Beginning-of-tier rectangle.
BLOCK 6 Middle-of-tier rectangle.
BLOCK 7 End-of-tier rectangle.

BOTTOM TIER, COLOR A
BLOCK 8 Beginning-of-tier rectangle.
BLOCKS 9–10 Middle-of-tier rectangles.
BLOCK 11 End-of-tier rectangle.

LEFT SIDE TIER, COLOR B
BLOCK 12 Beginning-of-tier rectangle.
BLOCK 13 Middle-of-tier rectangle.
BLOCK 14 End-of-round rectangle.

ROUND 5 With Colors C and B, working counterclockwise, follow Chart A on page 10.

LEFT SIDE TIER, COLOR C
BLOCK 1 Beginning-of-round rectangle with bind-off.
BLOCKS 2–3 Middle-of-tier rectangles with bind-off.
BLOCK 4 End-of-tier rectangle with bind-off.

BOTTOM TIER, COLOR B
BLOCK 5 Beginning-of-tier rectangle.
BLOCKS 6–8 Middle-of-tier rectangles.
BLOCK 9 End-of-tier rectangle.

RIGHT SIDE TIER, COLOR C
BLOCK 10 Beginning-of-tier rectangle with bind-off.
BLOCKS 11–12 Middle-of-tier rectangles with bind-off.
BLOCK 13 End-of-tier rectangle with bind-off.

TOP TIER, COLOR B

BLOCK 14 Beginning-of-tier rectangle.
BLOCKS 15–17 Middle-of-tier rectangles.
BLOCK 18 End-of-round rectangle.

ROUND 6 With Color C, working clockwise, follow Chart B on page 11.

TOP TIER, COLOR C

BLOCK 1 Cast-on rectangle with bind-off.
BLOCKS 2–5 Middle-of-tier rectangles with bind-off.
BLOCK 6 End-of-tier rectangle with bind-off.

BOTTOM TIER, COLOR C

BLOCK 7 Cast-on rectangle with bind-off.
BLOCKS 8–11 Middle-of-tier rectangles with bind-off.
BLOCK 12 End-of-tier rectangle with bind-off.

FINISHING

Sew in ends. See Appendix, Entrelac Tips, Terms and Techniques, Sewing in Ends, for tips on how to have a neatly finished edge. Wash and block.

8 PLACEMAT/TOWEL

Add a splash of color to your table, or make an adsorbent towel to complement your kitchen.

The placemat/towel is worked in stockinette, with 6 stitch blocks. Chart A and Chart B refer to the mitered entrelac technique charts on pages 10 and 11. (Figure 1)

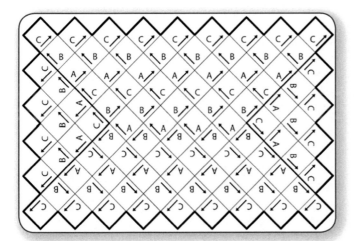

FIGURE 1 Placemat/Towel Diagram

Finished Measurements
11" x 17"

Materials
- Lily Sugar'n Cream Ombres & Prints (100% cotton; 95 yards per 57 gram skein)
  - [Color A] Summer Splash #1211; 1 skein, uses approximately 40 yards
- Lily Sugar'n Cream Solids & Denim (100% cotton; 200 yards per 115 gram skein)
  - [Color B] Hot Green #18712; 1 skein, uses approximately 60 yards
  - [Color C] Mod Blue #18111; 1 skein, uses approximately 75 yards
- 32–40-inch US #7/4.5mm circular needle, or size needed to obtain gauge

Gauge
18 stitches and 28 rows = 4"/10 cm in stockinette stitch. Gauge is not critical in this pattern, but a different gauge will affect yardage and size of finished item.

ROUND 1 Placemat/Towel Diagram Center row, working counterclockwise (from right to left), with Color A, follow Chart A on page 10. (Figure 2)

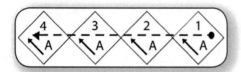

FIGURE 2 Round 1

BLOCKS 1–4 Center-row-setup rectangles; only provisionally cast on the stitches for one block at a time.

ROUND 2 With Colors B and C, working clockwise (from left to right), follow Chart B on page 11. (Figure 3)

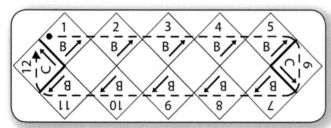

FIGURE 3 Round 2

TOP TIER, COLOR B
BLOCK 1 Beginning-of-round rectangle.
BLOCKS 2–4 Middle-of-tier rectangles.
BLOCK 5 End-of-tier rectangle.

RIGHT SIDE TIER, COLOR C
BLOCK 6 Beginning- and end-of-tier rectangle.

BOTTOM TIER, COLOR B
BLOCK 7 Beginning-of-tier rectangle.
BLOCKS 8–10 Middle-of-tier rectangles. Note that for blocks 8–11, you will be picking up stitches from the bottom to the top of the entrelac block below; not top to bottom as normal.
BLOCK 11 End-of-tier rectangle.

LEFT SIDE TIER, COLOR C
BLOCK 12 Beginning-of-tier and end-of-round combined rectangle.

ROUND 3 With Colors A and C, working counter-clockwise, follow Chart A on page 10. (Figure 4)

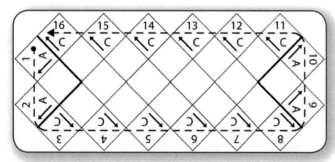

FIGURE 4 Round 3

LEFT SIDE TIER, COLOR A
BLOCK 1 Beginning-of-round rectangle.
BLOCK 2 End-of-tier rectangle.

BOTTOM TIER, COLOR C
BLOCK 3 Beginning-of-tier rectangle.
BLOCKS 4–7 Middle-of-tier rectangles.
BLOCK 8 End-of-tier rectangle.

RIGHT SIDE TIER, COLOR A
BLOCK 9 Beginning-of-tier rectangle.
BLOCK 10 End-of-tier rectangle.

TOP TIER, COLOR C
BLOCK 11 Beginning-of-tier rectangle.
BLOCKS 12–15 Middle-of-tier rectangles.
BLOCK 16 End-of-round rectangle.

ROUND 4 With Colors A and B, working clockwise, follow Chart B on page 11. (Figure 5)

TOP TIER, COLOR A
BLOCK 1 Beginning-of-round rectangle.
BLOCKS 2–6 Middle-of-tier rectangles.
BLOCK 7 End-of-tier rectangle.

RIGHT SIDE TIER, COLOR B
BLOCK 8 Beginning-of-tier rectangle.
BLOCK 9 Middle-of-tier rectangle.
BLOCK 10 End-of-tier rectangle.

BOTTOM TIER, COLOR A
BLOCK 11 Beginning-of-tier rectangle.
BLOCKS 12–16 Middle-of-tier rectangles.
BLOCK 17 End-of-tier rectangle.

LEFT SIDE TIER, COLOR B
BLOCK 18 Beginning-of-tier rectangle.
BLOCK 19 Middle-of-tier rectangle.
BLOCK 20 End-of-round rectangle.

ROUND 5 With Colors C and B, working counter-clockwise, follow Chart A on page 10.

LEFT SIDE TIER, COLOR C
BLOCK 1 Beginning-of-round rectangle with bind-off.
BLOCKS 2–3 Middle-of-tier rectangles with bind-off.
BLOCK 4 End-of-tier rectangle with bind-off.

BOTTOM TIER, COLOR B
BLOCK 5 Beginning-of-tier rectangle.
BLOCKS 6–11 Middle-of-tier rectangles.
BLOCK 12 End-of-tier rectangle.

RIGHT SIDE TIER, COLOR C
BLOCK 13 Beginning-of-tier rectangle with bind-off.
BLOCKS 14–15 Middle-of-tier rectangles with bind-off.
BLOCK 16 End-of-tier rectangle with bind-off.

TOP TIER, COLOR B
BLOCK 17 Beginning-of-tier rectangle.
BLOCKS 18–23 Middle-of-tier rectangles.
BLOCK 24 End-of-round rectangle.

ROUND 6 With Color C, working clockwise, follow Chart B on page 11.

TOP TIER, COLOR C

BLOCK 1 Cast-on rectangle with bind-off.
BLOCKS 2–8 Middle-of-tier rectangles with bind-off.
BLOCK 9 End-of-tier rectangle with bind-off.

BOTTOM TIER, COLOR C

BLOCK 10 Cast-on rectangle with bind-off.
BLOCKS 11–17 Middle-of-tier rectangles with bind-off.
BLOCK 18 End-of-tier rectangle with bind-off.

FINISHING

Sew in ends. See Appendix, Entrelac Tips, Terms and Techniques, Sewing in Ends, for tips on how to have a neatly finished edge. Wash and block.

Finished Measurements
4.5" x 4.5"

Materials

◇ Lily Sugar'n Cream Ombres & Prints (100% cotton; 95 yards per 57 gram skein)
- [Color A] Summer Splash #1211; 1 skein, uses approximately 2 yards

◇ Lily Sugar'n Cream Solids & Denim (100% cotton; 200 yards per 115 gram skein)
- [Color B] Hot Green #18712; 1 skein, uses approximately 8 yards
- [Color C] Mod Blue#18111; 1 skein, uses approximately 16 yards

◇ 32–40-inch US #7 / 4.5mm circular needle, or size needed to obtain gauge

Gauge
18 stitches and 28 rows = 4"/10 cm in stockinette stitch. Gauge is not critical in this pattern, but a different gauge will affect yardage and size of finished item.

9 COASTER

Just a little cotton will make many coasters for your home or as a thoughtful gift.

The coaster is worked in stockinette, with 5 stitch blocks. Chart A and Chart B refer to the mitered entrelac technique charts on pages 10 and 11. (Figure 1)

ROUND 1 Center row, working counterclockwise (from right to left), with Color A, follow Chart A on page 10. (Figure 2)

BLOCK 1 Center-row-setup rectangle.

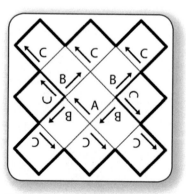

FIGURE 1 Coaster Diagram

FIGURE 2 Round 1

ROUND 2 With Colors B and C, working clockwise (from left to right), follow Chart B on page 11. (Figure 3)

TOP TIER, COLOR B

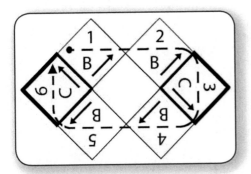

FIGURE 3 Round 2

BLOCK 1 Beginning-of-round rectangle.
BLOCK 2 End-of-tier rectangle.

RIGHT SIDE TIER, COLOR C
BLOCK 3 Beginning- and end-of-tier rectangle with bind-off.

BOTTOM TIER, COLOR B
BLOCK 4 Beginning-of-tier rectangle.
BLOCK 5 End-of-tier rectangle. Note that for this block, you will be picking up stitches from the bottom to the top of the entrelac block below; not top to bottom as normal.

LEFT SIDE TIER, COLOR C
BLOCK 6 Beginning-of-tier and end-of-round combined rectangle with bind-off.

ROUND 3 With Color C, working counterclockwise, follow Chart A on page 10. (Figure 4)

BOTTOM TIER, COLOR C
BLOCK 1 Cast-on rectangle with bind-off.

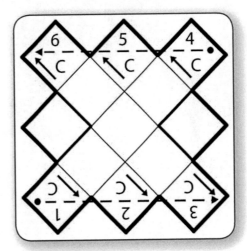

FIGURE 4 Round 3

BLOCK 2 Middle-of-tier rectangle with bind-off .
BLOCK 3 End-of-tier rectangle with bind-off.

TOP TIER, COLOR C
BLOCK 4 Cast-on rectangle with bind-off.
BLOCK 5 Middle-of-tier rectangle with bind-off .
BLOCK 6 End-of-tier rectangle with bind-off.

FINISHING

Sew in ends. See Appendix, Entrelac Tips, Terms and Techniques, Sewing in Ends, for tips on how to have a neatly finished edge. Wash and block.

10 TRIVET/POTHOLDER

Finished Measurements
7.5" x 7.5"

Materials
- Lily Sugar'n Cream Ombres & Prints (100% cotton; 95 yards per 57 gram skein)
  - [Color A] Summer Splash #1211; 1 skein, uses approximately 15 yards
- Lily Sugar'n Cream Solids & Denim (100% cotton; 200 yards per 115 gram skein)
  - [Color B] Hot Green #18712; 1 skein, uses approximately 30 yards
  - [Color C] Mod Blue#18111; 1 skein, uses approximately 50 yards
- 32–40-inch US #7 / 4.5mm circular needle, or size needed to obtain gauge

Gauge
18 stitches and 20 rows = 4"/10 cm in with yarn doubled in k1, p1 ribbing. Gauge is not critical in this pattern, but a different gauge will affect yardage and size of finished item.

The potholder may be worked with an optional buttonhole extension if you wish to hang it in your kitchen.

The trivet/potholder is worked with 5 stitch ribbed blocks with yarn doubled. See Chapter 5, Working Ribbed Blocks. Chart A and Chart B refer to the mitered entrelac technique charts on pages 10 and 11. (Figure 1)

ROUND 1 Center row, working counterclockwise (from right to left), with Color C, follow Chart A on page 10. (Figure 2)

BLOCK 1 Center-row-setup rectangle.

ROUND 2 With Colors A and B, working clockwise (from left to right), follow Chart B on page 11. (Figure 3)

TOP TIER, COLOR A
BLOCK 1 Beginning-of-round rectangle.
BLOCK 2 End-of-tier rectangle.

RIGHT SIDE TIER, COLOR B
BLOCK 3 Beginning- and end-of-tier rectangle.

BOTTOM TIER, COLOR A
BLOCK 4 Beginning-of-tier rectangle.
BLOCK 5 End-of-tier rectangle. Note that for this block, you will be picking up stitches from the bottom to the top of the entrelac block below; not top to bottom as normal.

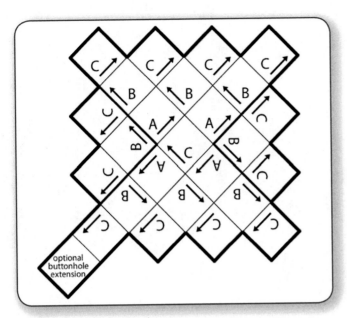

FIGURE 1 Trivet/Potholder diagram

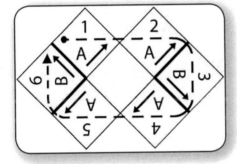

FIGURE 2 Round 1   **FIGURE 3** Round 2

LEFT SIDE TIER, COLOR B

BLOCK 6 Beginning-of-tier and end-of-round combined rectangle.

ROUND 3 With Colors C and B, working counter-clockwise, follow Chart A on page 10. (Figure 4)

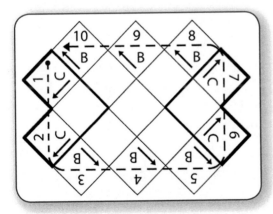

FIGURE 4 Round 3

LEFT SIDE TIER, COLOR C

BLOCK 1 Beginning-of-round rectangle with bind-off.
BLOCK 2 End-of-tier rectangle with bind-off.

BOTTOM TIER, COLOR B

BLOCK 3 Beginning-of-tier rectangle.
BLOCK 4 Middle-of-tier rectangle.
BLOCK 5 End-of-tier rectangle.

RIGHT SIDE TIER, COLOR C

BLOCK 6 Beginning-of-tier rectangle with bind-off.
BLOCK 7 End-of-tier rectangle with bind-off.

TOP TIER, COLOR B

BLOCK 8 Beginning-of-tier rectangle.
BLOCK 9 Middle-of-tier rectangle.
BLOCK 10 End-of-round rectangle.

ROUND 4 With Color C, working clockwise, follow Chart B on page 11.

TOP TIER, COLOR C

BLOCK 1 Cast-on rectangle with bind-off.
BLOCKS 2–3 Middle-of-tier rectangles with bind-off.
BLOCK 4 End-of-tier rectangle with bind-off.

BOTTOM TIER, COLOR C

BLOCK 5 Cast-on rectangle with bind-off.
BLOCKS 6–7 Middle-of-tier rectangles with bind-off.
BLOCK 8 End-of-tier rectangle with optional buttonhole extension and bind-off. For Trivet, work block 8 same as block 4. For Potholder, add optional buttonhole extension if desired for hanging. Work optional buttonhole extension as follows: Do not bind off on row 10; work 4 additional rows; work buttonhole; work 4 more rows (19 rows total in block). Bind off. Sew button on bottom half of block.

FINISHING

Sew in ends. See Appendix, Entrelac Tips, Terms and Techniques, Sewing in Ends, for tips on how to have a neatly finished edge. Wash and block.

11 RAINBOW SHERBET BABY BLANKET

Wrap your favorite baby or toddler in a rainbow of love.

The blanket is worked in stockinette, with 8 stitch blocks. Chart A and Chart B refer to the mitered entrelac technique charts on pages 10 and 21. (Figure 1)

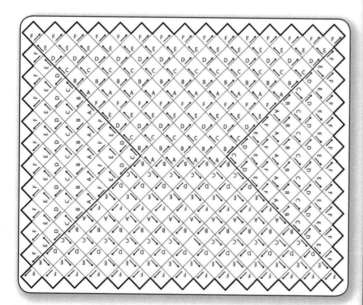

FIGURE 1 Blanket Diagram

Finished Measurements
28" x 34"

Materials
Cascade 220 Superwash
(100% wool; 220 yards per 100 gram skein)
[Color A] Flamingo #903; approximately 102 yards
[Color B] Tangerine #826; approximately 120 yards
[Color C] Lemon #820; approximately 145 yards
[Color D] Lime #851; approximately 170 yards
[Color E] Turquoise #812; approximately 190 yards
[Color F] Amethyst #804; approximately 215 yards
47–60-inch US #7 / 4.5mm circular needle, or size needed to obtain gauge

Gauge
20 stitches and 30 rows = 4"/10 cm in stockinette stitch. Gauge is not critical in this pattern, but a different gauge will affect yardage and size of finished item.

ROUND 1 Center row, working counterclockwise (from right to left), with Color A, follow Chart A on page 10 (Figure 2).

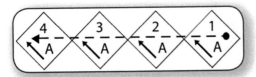

FIGURE 2 Round 1

BLOCKS 1–4 Center-row-setup rectangles; only provisionally cast on the stitches for one block at a time.

ROUND 2 With Colors B and C, working clockwise (from left to right), follow Chart B on page 11 (Figure 3).

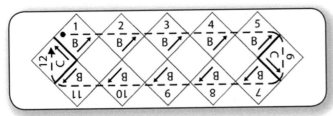

FIGURE 3 Round 2

TOP TIER, COLOR B
BLOCK 1 Beginning-of-round rectangle.
BLOCKS 2–4 Middle-of-tier rectangles.
BLOCK 5 End-of-tier rectangle.

RIGHT SIDE TIER, COLOR C
BLOCK 6 Beginning- and end-of-tier combined rectangle.

BOTTOM TIER, COLOR B
BLOCK 7 Beginning-of-tier rectangle.
BLOCKS 8–10 Middle-of-tier rectangles. Note that for blocks 8–11, you will be picking up stitches from the bottom to the top of the entrelac block below; not top to bottom as normal.
BLOCK 11 End-of-tier rectangle.

LEFT SIDE TIER, COLOR C
BLOCK 12 Beginning-of-tier and end-of-round combined rectangle.

ROUND 3 With Colors D and C, working counter-clockwise, follow Chart A on page 10. (Figure 4)

FIGURE 4 Round 3

LEFT SIDE TIER, COLOR D
BLOCK 1 Beginning-of-round rectangle.
BLOCK 2 End-of-tier rectangle.

BOTTOM TIER, COLOR C
BLOCK 3 Beginning-of-tier rectangle.
BLOCKS 4–7 Middle-of-tier rectangles.
BLOCK 8 End-of-tier rectangle.

RIGHT SIDE TIER, COLOR D
BLOCK 9 Beginning-of-tier rectangle.
BLOCK 10 End-of-tier rectangle.

TOP TIER, COLOR C
BLOCK 11 Beginning-of-tier rectangle.
BLOCKS 12–15 Middle-of-tier rectangles.
BLOCK 16 End-of-round rectangle.

ROUND 4 With Colors D and E, working clockwise, follow Chart B on page 11.

TOP TIER, COLOR D
BLOCK 1 Beginning-of-round rectangle.
BLOCKS 2–6 Middle-of-tier rectangles.
BLOCK 7 End-of-tier rectangle.

RIGHT SIDE TIER, COLOR E
BLOCK 8 Beginning-of-tier rectangle.
BLOCK 9 Middle-of-tier rectangle.
BLOCK 10 End-of-tier rectangle.

BOTTOM TIER, COLOR D
BLOCK 11 Beginning-of-tier rectangle.
BLOCKS 12–16 Middle-of-tier rectangles.
BLOCK 17 End-of-tier rectangle.

LEFT SIDE TIER, COLOR E
BLOCK 18 Beginning-of-tier rectangle.
BLOCK 19 Middle-of-tier rectangle.
BLOCK 20 End-of-round rectangle.

ROUND 5 With Colors F and E, working counter-clockwise, follow Chart A on page 10.

LEFT SIDE TIER, COLOR F
BLOCK 1 Beginning-of-round rectangle.
BLOCKS 2–3 Middle-of-tier rectangles.
BLOCK 4 End-of-tier rectangle.

BOTTOM TIER, COLOR E
BLOCK 5 Beginning-of-tier rectangle.
BLOCKS 6–11 Middle-of-tier rectangles.
BLOCK 12 End-of-tier rectangle.

RIGHT SIDE TIER, COLOR F
BLOCK 13 Beginning-of-tier rectangle.
BLOCKS 14–15 Middle-of-tier rectangles.
BLOCK 16 End-of-tier rectangle.

TOP TIER, COLOR E
BLOCK 17 Beginning-of-tier rectangle.
BLOCKS 18–23 Middle-of-tier rectangles.
BLOCK 24 End-of-round rectangle.

ROUND 6 With Colors F and A, working clockwise, follow Chart B on page 11.

TOP TIER, COLOR F
BLOCK 1 Beginning-of-round rectangle.
BLOCKS 2–8 Middle-of-tier rectangles.
BLOCK 9 End-of-tier rectangle.

RIGHT SIDE TIER, COLOR A
BLOCK 10 Beginning-of-tier rectangle.
BLOCKS 11–13 Middle-of-tier rectangles.
BLOCK 14 End-of-tier rectangle.

BOTTOM TIER, COLOR F
BLOCK 15 Beginning-of-tier rectangle.
BLOCKS 16–22 Middle-of-tier rectangles.
BLOCK 23 End-of-tier rectangle.

LEFT SIDE TIER, COLOR A
BLOCK 24 Beginning-of-tier rectangle.
BLOCKS 25–27 Middle-of-tier rectangles.
BLOCK 28 End-of-round rectangle.

ROUND 7 With Colors B and A, working counter-clockwise, follow Chart A on page 10.

LEFT SIDE TIER, COLOR B
BLOCK 1 Beginning-of-round rectangle.
BLOCKS 2–5 Middle-of-tier rectangles.
BLOCK 6 End-of-tier rectangle.

BOTTOM TIER, COLOR A
BLOCK 7 Beginning-of-tier rectangle.
BLOCKS 8–15 Middle-of-tier rectangles.
BLOCK 16 End-of-tier rectangle.

RIGHT SIDE TIER, COLOR B
BLOCK 17 Beginning-of-tier rectangle.
BLOCKS 18–21 Middle-of-tier rectangles.
BLOCK 22 End-of-tier rectangle.

TOP TIER, COLOR A
BLOCK 23 Beginning-of-tier rectangle.
BLOCKS 24–31 Middle-of-tier rectangles.
BLOCK 32 End-of-round rectangle.

ROUND 8 With Colors B and C, working clockwise, follow Chart B on page 11.

TOP TIER, COLOR B
BLOCK 1 Beginning-of-round rectangle.
BLOCKS 2–10 Middle-of-tier rectangles.
BLOCK 11 End-of-tier rectangle.

RIGHT SIDE TIER, COLOR C
BLOCK 12 Beginning-of-tier rectangle.
BLOCKS 13–17 Middle-of-tier rectangles.
BLOCK 18 End-of-tier rectangle.

BOTTOM TIER, COLOR B
BLOCK 19 Beginning-of-tier rectangle.

BLOCKS 20–28 Middle-of-tier rectangles.
BLOCK 29 End-of-tier rectangle.

LEFT SIDE TIER, COLOR C
BLOCK 30 Beginning-of-tier rectangle.
BLOCKS 31–35 Middle-of-tier rectangles.
BLOCK 36 End-of-round rectangle.

ROUND 9 With Colors D and C, working counter-clockwise, follow Chart A on page 10.

LEFT SIDE TIER, COLOR D
BLOCK 1 Beginning-of-round rectangle.
BLOCKS 2–7 Middle-of-tier rectangles.
BLOCK 8 End-of-tier rectangle.

BOTTOM TIER, COLOR C
BLOCK 9 Beginning-of-tier rectangle.
BLOCKS 10–19 Middle-of-tier rectangles.
BLOCK 20 End-of-tier rectangle.

RIGHT SIDE TIER, COLOR D
BLOCK 21 Beginning-of-tier rectangle.
BLOCKS 22–27 Middle-of-tier rectangles.
BLOCK 28 End-of-tier rectangle.

TOP TIER, COLOR C
BLOCK 29 Beginning-of-tier rectangle.
BLOCKS 30–39 Middle-of-tier rectangles.
BLOCK 40 End-of-round rectangle.

ROUND 10 With Colors D and E, working clockwise, follow Chart B on page 11.

TOP TIER, COLOR D
BLOCK 1 Beginning-of-round rectangle.
BLOCKS 2–12 Middle-of-tier rectangles.
BLOCK 13 End-of-tier rectangle.

RIGHT SIDE TIER, COLOR E
BLOCK 14 Beginning-of-tier rectangle.
BLOCKS 15–21 Middle-of-tier rectangles.
BLOCK 22 End-of-tier rectangle.

BOTTOM TIER, COLOR D
BLOCK 23 Beginning-of-tier rectangle.
BLOCKS 24–34 Middle-of-tier rectangles.
BLOCK 35 End-of-tier rectangle.

LEFT SIDE TIER, COLOR E
BLOCK 36 Beginning-of-tier rectangle.
BLOCKS 37–43 Middle-of-tier rectangles.
BLOCK 44 End-of-round rectangle.

ROUND 11 With Colors F and E, working counter-clockwise, follow Chart A on page 10.

LEFT SIDE TIER, COLOR F
BLOCK 1 Beginning-of-round rectangle with bind-off.
BLOCKS 2–9 Middle-of-tier rectangles with bind-off.
BLOCK 10 End-of-tier rectangle with bind-off.

BOTTOM TIER, COLOR E

BLOCK 11 Beginning-of-tier rectangle.

BLOCKS 12–23 Middle-of-tier rectangles.

BLOCK 24 End-of-tier rectangle.

RIGHT SIDE TIER, COLOR F

BLOCK 25 Beginning-of-tier rectangle with bind-off.

BLOCKS 26–33 Middle-of-tier rectangles with bind-off.

BLOCK 34 End-of-tier rectangle with bind-off.

TOP TIER, COLOR E

BLOCK 35 Beginning-of-tier rectangle.

BLOCKS 36–47 Middle-of-tier rectangles.

BLOCK 48 End-of-round rectangle.

ROUND 12 With Color F, working clockwise, follow Chart B on page 11.

TOP TIER, COLOR F

BLOCK 1 Cast-on rectangle with bind-off.

BLOCKS 2–14 Middle-of-tier rectangles with bind-off.

BLOCK 15 End-of-tier rectangle with bind-off.

BOTTOM TIER, COLOR F

BLOCK 16 Cast-on rectangle with bind-off.

BLOCKS 17–29 Middle-of-tier rectangles with bind-off.

BLOCK 30 End-of-tier rectangle with bind-off.

FINISHING

Sew in ends. See Appendix, Entrelac Tips, Terms and Techniques, Sewing in Ends, for tips on how to have a neatly finished edge. Wash and block.

Finished Measurements

blanket, 14" x 14"; bunny head, 8" circumference; ears, 6.5" long.

Materials

✧ Cascade 220 Superwash (100% wool; 220 yards
   per 100 gram skein)
   • [Color A] Flamingo #903; approximately 140 yards
   • [Color B] Tangerine #826; approximately 110 yards
   • [Color C] Lemon #820; approximately 88 yards
   • [Color D] Lime #851; approximately 55 yards
   • [Color E] Turquoise #812; approximately 35 yards
   • [Color F] Amethyst #804; approximately 20 yards
✧ Washable polyester stuffing for bunny's head
✧ Embroidery thread for bunny's face
✧ 24–40-inch US #7/4.5mm circular needle, or size needed to obtain gauge
✧ 20–29-inch US #4/3.5mm circular needle, or size needed to obtain gauge, for bunny head, 2 circulars or dpns may be used if preferred.

Gauge

20 stitches and 30 rows = 4"/10 cm in stockinette stitch on larger needles. Gauge is not critical in this pattern, but a different gauge will affect yardage and size of finished item.

12 BUNNY LOVEY

The Bunny Lovey complements the Rainbow Sherbet Baby Blanket and is designed to use the leftover yarn. The colors are used in reverse order.

The lovey blanket is worked in stockinette, with 7 stitch blocks and larger needles. The blanket has a hole in the center where you will add the bunny's head later. (Figure 1) Round 1 is worked like any project that is cast on and joined to work in the round. Round 2 will begin the mitered entrelac, but some of the blocks will be modified to work from circular round 1. Beginning with round 3, you will be working basic mitered entrelac. Chart A and Chart B refer to the mitered entrelac technique charts on pages 10 and 11.

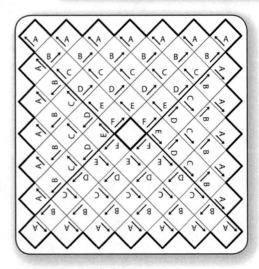

FIGURE 1 *Lovely Blanket Diagram*

ROUND 1 Using Color F, cast on 28 stitches. Being careful not to twist, join in a circle and knit one round.

ROUND 2 With Colors F and E, working clockwise (from left to right), follow Chart B on page 11. (Figure 2)

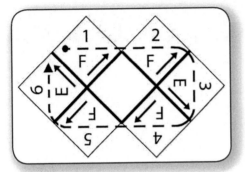

FIGURE 2 Blanket Round 2

TOP TIER, COLOR F
BLOCK 1 Work as a beginning-of-round rectangle, except, with working yarn, provisionally cast on 7 stitches onto needle with stitches just worked. Omit the first (knit) row, and begin with the second (purl) row. The p2togs will attach or join the last 7 stitches of round 1.
BLOCK 2 Work as an end-of-tier rectangle, using the next 7 stitches from round 1 instead of casting on. Omit the first (knit) row, and begin with the second (purl) row.

RIGHT SIDE TIER, COLOR E
BLOCK 3 Beginning- and end-of-tier rectangle.

BOTTOM TIER, COLOR F
BLOCK 4 Beginning-of-tier rectangle. The p2togs will attach or join the next 7 stitches of round 1.
BLOCK 5 Same as block 2, earlier in round 2.

LEFT SIDE TIER, COLOR E
BLOCK 6 Beginning-of-tier and end-of-round combined rectangle.

ROUND 3 With Colors D and E, working counter-clockwise, follow Chart A on page 10. (Figure 3)

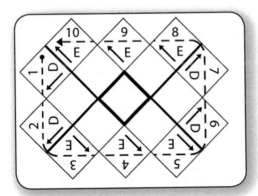

FIGURE 3 Blanket Round 3

LEFT SIDE TIER, COLOR D
BLOCK 1 Beginning-of-round rectangle.
BLOCK 2 End-of-tier rectangle.

BOTTOM TIER, COLOR E
BLOCK 3 Beginning-of-tier rectangle.
BLOCK 4 Middle-of-tier rectangle.
BLOCK 5 End-of-tier rectangle.

RIGHT SIDE TIER, COLOR D
BLOCK 6 Beginning-of-tier rectangle.
BLOCK 7 End-of-tier rectangle.

TOP TIER, COLOR E
BLOCK 8 Beginning-of-tier rectangle.
BLOCK 9 Middle-of-tier rectangle.
BLOCK 10 End-of-round rectangle.

ROUND 4 With Colors D and C, working clockwise, follow Chart B on page 11.

TOP TIER, COLOR D
BLOCK 1 Beginning-of-round rectangle.
BLOCKS 2–3 Middle-of-tier rectangles.
BLOCK 4 End-of-tier rectangle.

RIGHT SIDE TIER, COLOR C
BLOCK 5 Beginning-of-tier rectangle.
BLOCK 6 Middle-of-tier rectangle.
BLOCK 7 End-of-tier rectangle.

BOTTOM TIER, COLOR D
BLOCK 8 Beginning-of-tier rectangle.
BLOCKS 9–10 Middle-of-tier rectangles.
BLOCK 11 End-of-tier rectangle.

LEFT SIDE TIER, COLOR C
BLOCK 12 Beginning-of-tier rectangle.
BLOCK 13 Middle-of-tier rectangle.
BLOCK 14 End-of-round rectangle.

ROUND 5 With Colors B and C, working counter-clockwise, follow Chart A on page 10.

LEFT SIDE TIER, COLOR B
BLOCK 1 Beginning-of-round rectangle.
BLOCKS 2–3 Middle-of-tier rectangles.
BLOCK 4 End-of-tier rectangle.

BOTTOM TIER, COLOR C
BLOCK 5 Beginning-of-tier rectangle.
BLOCKS 6–8 Middle-of-tier rectangles.
BLOCK 9 End-of-tier rectangle.

RIGHT SIDE TIER, COLOR B
BLOCK 10 Beginning-of-tier rectangle.
BLOCKS 11–12 Middle-of-tier rectangles.
BLOCK 13 End-of-tier rectangle.

TOP TIER, COLOR C
BLOCK 14 Beginning-of-tier rectangle.
BLOCKS 15-17 Middle-of-tier rectangles.
BLOCK 18 End-of-round rectangle.

ROUND 6 With Colors B and A, working clockwise, follow Chart B on page 11.

TOP TIER, COLOR B
BLOCK 1 Beginning-of-round rectangle.
BLOCKS 2–5 Middle-of-tier rectangles.
BLOCK 6 End-of-tier rectangle.

RIGHT SIDE TIER, COLOR A
BLOCK 7 Beginning-of-tier rectangle with bind-off.
BLOCKS 8–10 Middle-of-tier rectangles with bind-off.
BLOCK 11 End-of-tier rectangle with bind-off.

BOTTOM TIER, COLOR B
BLOCK 12 Beginning-of-tier rectangle.
BLOCKS 13–16 Middle-of-tier rectangles.
BLOCK 17 End-of-tier rectangle.

LEFT SIDE TIER, COLOR A
BLOCK 18 Beginning-of-tier rectangle with bind-off.
BLOCKS 19–21 Middle-of-tier rectangles with bind-off.
BLOCK 22 End-of-round rectangle with bind-off.

ROUND 7 With Color A, working counterclockwise, follow Chart A on page 10.

TOP TIER, COLOR A
BLOCK 1 Cast-on rectangle with bind-off.
BLOCKS 2–6 Middle-of-tier rectangles with bind-off.
BLOCK 7 End-of-tier rectangle with bind-off.

BOTTOM TIER, COLOR A
BLOCK 8 Cast-on rectangle with bind-off.
BLOCKS 9–13 Middle-of-tier rectangles with bind-off.
BLOCK 14 End-of-tier rectangle with bind-off.

The blanket, with a hole in middle, is now complete. It is possible to sew in ends and wash and block the blanket at this point. The rest of the lovey, while washable, does not need to be blocked, and as the head is stuffed, it will take longer to dry.

BUNNY HEAD

The bunny head will be knit in the round, using Color F and smaller needles. (Figure 4) Rounds will begin at the back of the head. Stitches will be picked up from the edge of the hole of the blanket, beginning in the middle of a wider side edge of a block (not a bottom edge).

Using Color A, and beginning in the middle of the first block of the blanket worked , round 2, block 1 (where your ends are), pick up 28 stitches, 7 in each of the 4 blocks, place marker. Marker is at back of bunny head.

Rounds 1, 2 (all rounds are RS): K28.
Round 3: K1, [m1R, k2] six times , [m1R, k1] two times, m1L, k1, [m1L, k2] six times, M1L. 44 sts.
Round 4: K44.

FIGURE 4 Bunny Head

Round 5: K21, [m1R, k1] two times, [m1L, k1] two times, k19. 48 sts.
Rounds 6–11: K48.
Round 12: K22, k2tog, k1, ssk, k21. 46 sts.
Round 13: K21, k2tog, k1, ssk, k20. 44 sts.
Round 14: K20, k2tog, k1, ssk, k19. 42 sts.
Rounds 15–24: k42.
Round 25: [K4, k2tog] seven times. 35 sts.
Round 26: K35.
Round 27: [K3, k2tog] seven times. 28 sts.
Round 28: K28.
Round 29: [K2, k2tog] seven times. 21 sts.
Round 30: K21.
Round 31: [K1, k2tog] seven times. 14 sts.
Round 32: [K2tog] seven times. 7 sts.

Cut yarn, leaving a 12" tail; draw tail through remaining stitches. Pull tail to inside of head and tighten. Sew in end securely.

BUNNY EARS

Bunny ears are entrelac in the round with two blocks in each round. The ear diagram shows the front view, and the back looks identical. Bunny ears are worked using larger needles, and shaping is accomplished by changing the sizes of the blocks. It is easiest to work with 3 dpns as shown for the purse strap in the purse pattern (pages 68 & 69).

When making toys, I prefer to pick up stitches for appendages, so that they cannot become detached and pose a choking hazard. It is possible work the ears separately and sew securely to head if you prefer. Because the size of the blocks change to shape the ears, the size of the block will be given in each round. For proper ear placement, it is helpful to stuff the bunny's head. Using the photo of the bunny's head (Figure 4, above) and the decrease lines worked at the top of the head as guides, with Color A, pick up 4 stitches for a triangle at the bottom of the bunny's ear, and then pick up 4 more stitches back-to-back for the other triangle behind.

ROUND 1 With Color A, working counterclockwise (from right to left), work 4-stitch base triangles.

BLOCKS 1–2 Base triangles. First base triangle is worked on first 4 stitches only; reserve additional 4 stitches for second triangle.

Row 1 (RS): K2, turn.
Row 2 (WS): Sl1p, p1, turn.
Row 3: Sl1k, k2, turn.
Row 4: Sl1p, p2, turn.
Row 5: Sl1k, k3, turn.
Row 6: Sl1p, p3, turn.
Row 7: Sl1k, k3, do not turn.

Second base triangle is worked on 4 remaining picked-up stitches, using same directions.

ROUND 2 With Color B, working clockwise (from left to right), follow Chart B on page 11, working 4-stitch rectangles.
BLOCKS 1–2 Middle-of-tier rectangles.

ROUND 3 With Color C, working counterclockwise, follow Chart A on page 10, working 4-stitch rectangles.
BLOCKS 1–2 Middle-of-tier rectangles.

ROUND 4 With Color D, working clockwise, follow Chart B, working 4-stitch rectangles.
BLOCKS 1–2 Middle-of-tier rectangles.

ROUND 5 With Color E, working counterclockwise, follow Chart A on page 10, working 4-stitch rectangles.
Blocks 1–2; Middle-of-tier rectangles.

ROUND 6 With Color F, working clockwise, follow Chart B on page 11, transitioning from 4-stitch rectangles to 5-stitch rectangles.
BLOCKS 1–2 Modified-expanding middle-of-tier rectangles:

Pick up 4 stitches from rectangle below.

Rows 1, 3, 5, 7, 9 (RS): Sl1k, k3.
Rows 2, 4, (not 6), 8, 10 (WS): Sl1p, p2, P2tog last stitch of new color with next stitch of old color.
Row 6: Sl1p, p3.

ROUND 7 With Color A, working counterclockwise, follow Chart A on page 10, working 5-stitch rectangles.
BLOCKS 1-2 Middle-of-tier rectangles.

ROUND 8 With Color B, working clockwise, follow Chart B on page 11, working 5-stitch rectangles.
BLOCKS 1–2 Middle-of-tier rectangles.

ROUND 9 With Color C, working counterclockwise, follow Chart A on page 10, working 5-stitch rectangles.
BLOCKS 1–2 Middle-of-tier rectangles.

ROUND 10 With Color D, working clockwise, follow Chart B on page 11, transitioning from 5-stitch blocks to 4-stitch blocks.
BLOCKS 1–2 Modified-contracting-middle-of-tier rectangles:

Pick up 5 stitches from rectangle below.

Row 1(RS): Sl1k, k2tog, k2.
Rows 2, 4, (not 6), 8, 10 (WS): Sl1p, p2, p2tog last stitch of new color with next stitch of old color.
Rows 3, 5, 7, 9: Sl1k, k3.
Row 6: Sl1p, p2, p3tog last stitch of new color with next two stitches of old color.

ROUND 11 With Color E, working counterclockwise, follow Chart A on page 10, working 4-stitch blocks.
BLOCKS 1–2 Middle-of-tier rectangles with bind-off.

BUNNY FACE

Embroider bunny face as shown in photo. It may help to lightly stuff bunny head first. Before finishing lovey, remove stuffing and make sure all thread is securely tied inside bunny.

CLOSING BUNNY HEAD

Turn blanket upside down. Using larger needles and Color A, pick up 28 stitches around blanket hole, beginning at a corner between two blocks, place marker. Ideally these stitches are picked up into the bottom of the stitches that were picked up for the bunny head. Stuff bunny head. You may want to add additional stuffing as you are closing the bunny.

Round 1: [K5, k2tog] 4 times. 24 sts.
Round 2 and even rounds: Knit all.

Round 3: [K4, k2tog] 4 times. 20 sts.
Round 5: [K3, k2tog] 4 times. 16 sts.
Round 7: [K2, k2tog] 4 times. 12 sts.
Round 9: [K1, k2tog] 4 times. 8 sts.
Round 11: [K2tog] 4 times. 4 sts.

Cut a 12 inch tail, and draw it though the remaining 4 stitches. Pull to close opening and sew securely.

FINISHING

Sew in ends. See Appendix, Entrelac Tips, Terms and Techniques, Sewing in Ends, for tips on how to have a neatly finished edge. Wash and block if not done when blanket completed.

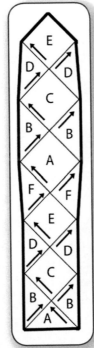

Finished Measurements

Length: 70", Width: 7"

Materials

✧ Berroco Ultra Alpaca (50% alpaca, 50% wool; 215 yards per 100 gram skein)
  • [MC] Navy #6243; 1 skein, uses approximately 206 yards
  • [CC1] Salt and Pepper #6207; 1 skein, uses approximately 120 yards
  • [CC2] Beet Root #6259; 1 skein, uses approximately 132 yards

✧ 47–60-inch US #6 / 4mm circular needle, or size needed to obtain gauge

Gauge

30 stitches and 32 rows = 4"/10 cm in k1, p1 ribbing.

The Folk Scarf is a stylish and warm winter accessory.

The folk scarf is a warm winter accessory made even cozier as a set with the folk mittens and hat. One skein of each color is enough to knit the scarf or the hat and mittens. To knit all three, you will need an additional skein of your main color, and will need to pay attention to which color is CC1, and which color is CC2. The scarf uses less of CC1, and more of CC2. The hat uses little of CC2, and more of CC1. Even the mittens use slightly more of CC2. If you wish to change the order of the contrast colors, you will probably need additional yarn.

The folk scarf is worked with 7 stitch ribbed blocks. See Chapter 5, Working Ribbed Blocks. Because of the length, it is easier to knit the top and one side of the scarf first, and then the bottom and other side. If you wish to do the complete round at the same time, you will need two long needles. Chart A and Chart B refer to the mitered entrelac technique charts on pages 10 and 11. (Figure 1)

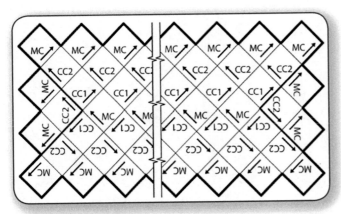

FIGURE 1 Scarf Diagram

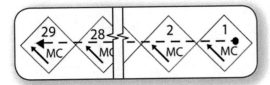

FIGURE 2 Round 1

INSTRUCTIONS

ROUND 1 With Color MC, working counterclockwise (from right to left), follow Chart A on page 10. (Figure 2)

BLOCKS 1–29 Center-row-setup rectangles; only provisionally cast on the stitches for one block at a time.

ROUND 2 (FIRST HALF) With Colors CC1 and CC2, working clockwise (from left to right), follow Chart B on page 11. (Figure 3)

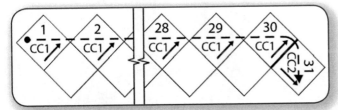

FIGURE 3 Round 2 (First Half)

TOP TIER, COLOR CC1
BLOCK 1 Beginning-of-round rectangle.
BLOCKS 2–29 Middle-of-tier rectangles.
BLOCK 30 End-of-tier rectangle.

RIGHT SIDE TIER, COLOR CC2
BLOCK 31 Beginning- and end-of-tier rectangle.

ROUND 3 (FIRST HALF) With Colors MC and CC2, working counterclockwise, follow Chart A on page 10. (Figure 4)

RIGHT SIDE TIER, COLOR MC
BLOCK 1 Beginning-of-round rectangle with bind-off.
BLOCK 2 End-of-tier rectangle with bind-off.

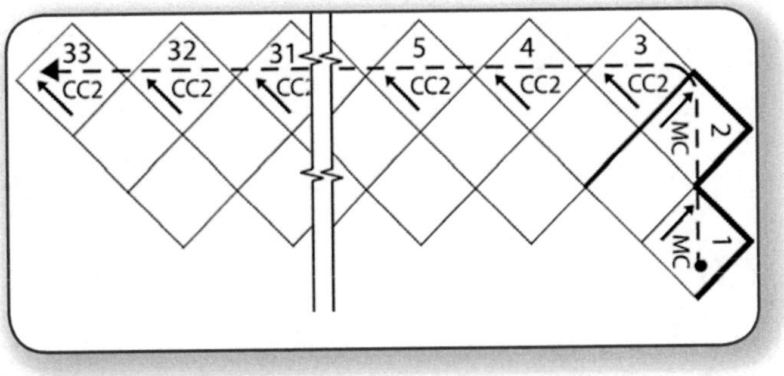

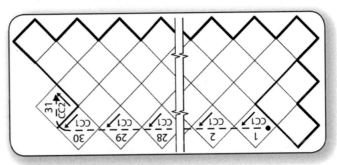

FIGURE 4 Round 3 (First Half)

TOP TIER, COLOR CC2
BLOCK 3 Beginning-of-tier rectangle.
BLOCKS 4–32 Middle-of-tier rectangles.
BLOCK 33 End-of-tier rectangle.

ROUND 4 (FIRST HALF) With Color MC, working clockwise, follow Chart B on page 11.

TOP TIER, COLOR MC
BLOCK 1 Cast-on rectangle with bind-off.
BLOCKS 2–31 Middle-of-tier rectangles with bind-off.
BLOCK 32 End-of-tier rectangle with bind-off.

ROUND 2 (SECOND HALF) With Colors CC1 and CC2, working clockwise (from left to right), follow Chart B on page 11. (Figure 5)

FIGURE 5 Round 2 (Second Half)

BOTTOM TIER, COLOR CC1
BLOCK 1 Beginning-of-tier rectangle.
BLOCKS 2–29 Middle-of-tier rectangles. Note that for blocks 2–30, you will be picking up stitches from the bottom to the top of the entrelac block below; not top to bottom as normal.
BLOCK 30 End-of-tier rectangle.

LEFT SIDE TIER, COLOR CC2
BLOCK 31 Beginning-of-tier and end-of-round combined rectangle.

ROUND 3 (SECOND HALF) With Colors MC and CC2, working counterclockwise, follow Chart A on page 10. (Figure 6)

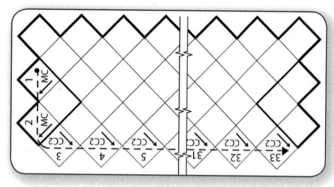

FIGURE 5 Round 3 (Second Half)

LEFT SIDE TIER, COLOR MC
BLOCK 1 Beginning-of-tier rectangle with bind-off.
BLOCK 2 End-of-tier rectangle with bind-off.

BOTTOM TIER, COLOR CC2
BLOCK 3 Beginning-of-tier rectangle.
BLOCKS 4–32 Middle-of-tier rectangles.
BLOCK 33 End-of-tier rectangle.

ROUND 4 (SECOND HALF) With Color MC, working clockwise, follow Chart B on page 11.

BOTTOM TIER, COLOR MC
BLOCK 1 Cast-on rectangle with bind-off.
BLOCKS 2–31 Middle-of-tier rectangles with bind-off.
BLOCK 32 End-of-tier rectangle with bind-off.

FINISHING

Sew in remaining ends. See Appendix, Entrelac Tips, Terms and Techniques, Sewing in Ends, for tips on how to have a neatly finished edge. Wash and block.

14 FOLK HAT

Finished Measurements
Sized to fit head circumferences:
20 (22, 24)"

Materials
- ✧ Berroco Ultra Alpaca (50% alpaca, 50% wool; 215 yards per 100 gram skein)
  - [MC] Navy #6243; 1 skein, uses approximately 95 (104, 113) yards
  - [CC1] Salt and Pepper #6207; 1 skein, uses approximately 36 (38, 40) yards
  - [CC2] Beet Root #6259; 1 skein, uses approximately 17 yards
- ✧ 2 16-inch US #6/4mm circular needles (one may be longer), or size needed to obtain gauge

Gauge
30 stitches and 32 rows = 4"/10 cm in k1, p1 ribbing.

The folk hat features mitered entrelac ear flaps, and makes a cozy winter set with the folk mittens and scarf.

This folk hat features mitered entrelac ear flaps. The rest of the hat is knit onto the ear flaps as a modified entrelac block, incorporating the flaps using entrelac-style attaching or joining. The ear flaps are worked with 7 stitch k1, p1 ribbed blocks. See Chapter 5, Working Ribbed Blocks. Chart A and Chart B refer to the mitered entrelac technique charts on pages 10 and 11.

One skein of each color is enough to knit the hat and mittens or the scarf. To knit all three, you will need an additional skein of your main color, and will need to pay attention to which color is CC1, and which color

is CC2. The scarf uses less of CC1, and more of CC2. The hat uses little of CC2, and more of CC1. Even the mittens use slightly more of CC2. If you wish to change the order of the contrast colors, or knit larger sizes, you will probably need additional yarn.

EAR FLAP INSTRUCTIONS

ROUND 1 Center row, working counterclockwise (from right to left), with Color MC, follow Chart A on page 10. (Figure 1)

BLOCK 1 Center-row-setup rectangle.

FIGURE 1
Round 1

ROUND 2 (FIRST HALF) With Colors CC2 and CC1, working clockwise (from left to right), follow Chart B on page 11. (Figure 2)

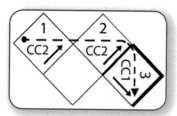

FIGURE 2 Round 2 (First Half)

TOP TIER, COLOR CC2
BLOCK 1 Beginning-of-round rectangle.
BLOCK 2 End-of-tier rectangle.

RIGHT SIDE TIER, COLOR CC1
BLOCK 3 Beginning- and end-of-tier rectangle with bind-off

ROUND 3 (FIRST HALF) With Color CC1, working counterclockwise, follow Chart A on page 10. (Figure 3)

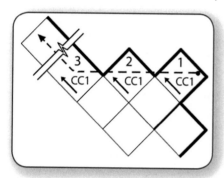

FIGURE 3 Round 3 (First Half)

TOP TIER, COLOR CC1
BLOCK 1 Cast-on rectangle with bind-off.
BLOCK 2 Middle-of-tier rectangle with cast off
BLOCK 3 Elongated end-of-tier rectangle (band). Following ribbing pattern, work 42 (46, 58) rows. After working final row, slip working stitches back to empty needle.

Using other circular needle, work a second partial ear flap identical to the first.

JOINING EAR FLAPS (FIGURE 4)

Rotate partial ear flaps, bands of hat, and needles as shown in Figure 4. The two pieces will be joined at point A. The first block will be worked with stitches picked up along the top edge of third block of round 2 (below A). At the right edge, stitches will be attached or joined from the first block of round 1 (the provisional cast-on). Simultaneously, at the left edge, stitches will be attached or joined from the third block (band) of round 3 on the other ear flap. Note that you will be working with needles attached to different cables.

ROUND 2 (SECOND HALF) With Colors CC2 and CC1, working clockwise, follow Chart B on page 11. (Figure 5)

LEFT SIDE TIER, COLOR CC2
BLOCK 1 Joining rectangle as follows: With WS facing (using needle in band), pick up 7 stitches purlwise along edge of block below point A (from round 2, block 3, CC1), turn.

Rows 1, 3, 5, 7, 9, 11, 13 (RS): Sl1k, p1, k1, p1, k1, p1, ssk with first stitch from band of other ear flap, turn.
Rows 2, 4, 6, 8, 10, 12, 14 (WS): Sl1p, k1, p1, k1, p1, k1, p2tog with first stitch from center block, turn except after row 14.

BLOCK 2 End-of-tier rectangle. Note that for block 2, you will be picking up stitches from the bottom to the top of the entrelac block below; not top to bottom as normal.

RIGHT SIDE TIER, COLOR CC1
BLOCK 3 Beginning-of-tier and end-of-round combined rectangle. After working final row, slip working stitches back to empty needle, and then down onto cable. Slide working stitches from block 2, recently worked, onto opposite needle to be joined in next round.

ROUND 3 (SECOND HALF) With Color CC1, working counterclockwise, follow Chart A on page 10. (Figure 6)

LEFT SIDE TIER, COLOR CC1
BLOCK 1 Beginning-of-round rectangle.
BLOCK 2 Middle-of-tier rectangle

Being careful not to twist, join other sides of the earflaps in the same manner.

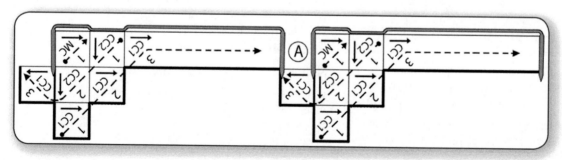

FIGURE 4
Joining Ear Flaps

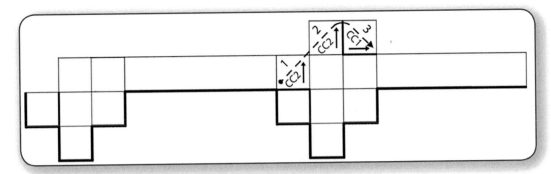

FIGURE 5
Round 2 (Second Half)

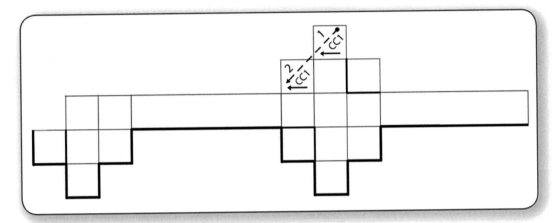

FIGURE 6
Round 3 (Second Half)

FILLING IN THE ENTRELAC

Remainder of hat will be worked with MC in k1, p1 ribbing. First the valleys between the tops of the flaps need to be filled in as large modified entrelac blocks. (Figure 7)

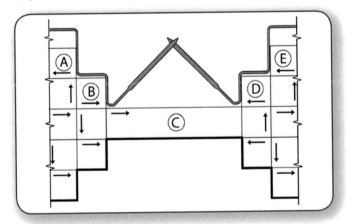

FIGURE 7 Filling In the Entrelac

With RS facing, and MC, pick up 21 (23, 29) stitches knitwise along top of block/band C, turn.

Row 1(WS): Sl1p, k1, [pfb, p1, kfb, k1] 4 (5, 6) times, [p1, k1] 0 (1, 0) times until last stitch, p2tog last stitch with first stitch from side of block D. 29 (33, 41) horizontal stitches total, not counting vertical stitches on side of blocks B and D waiting to be attached or joined, turn.

Rows 2, 4, 6, 8, 10, 12 (RS): Sl1k, [p1, k1] until last stitch, ssk with first stitch from side of block B, turn.
Rows 3, 5, 7, 9, 11: Sl1p, [k1, p1] until last stitch, p2tog with next stitch from side of block D, turn.
Row 13: Sl1p, [k1, p1] until last stitch, p2tog with last stitch from side of block D, do not turn, pick up 8 stitches purlwise along top edge of block D. 37 (41, 49) stitches total, turn. Note: It is necessary to pick up an even number of stitches here to maintain the ribbing and the joining; just pick up an extra stitch in the corner.
Row 14: Sl1k, [p1, k1] until last stitch, ssk with last stitch from side of block B, do not turn, pick up 8 stitches knitwise along top edge of block B, turn. 45 (49, 57) stitches total. The provisionally cast on stitches from Block A need to be mounted properly for attaching.
Rows 15, 17, 19, 21, 23, 25, 27: Sl1p, [k1, p1] until last stitch, p2tog with first stitch from side of block E, turn.
Rows 16, 18, 20, 22, 24, 26: Sl1k, [p1, k1] until last stitch, ssk with first stitch from side of block A, turn.
Row 28: Do not knit row 28 yet!

Fill in the second valley identically to the first, repeating rows 1–27.

Begin working in the round. Stitches may remain on two circular needles for crown decreases, or be worked on one 16" needle until crown is too small.

Round 28: Sl1k, [p1, k1] until last stitch, ssk with last stitch from side of block A, do not turn, pick up 7 stitches knitwise along top edge of block A, [k1, p1] until two stitches remain, one from ribbing, one from side of other top block, ssk, do not turn, pick up 3 stitches knitwise, place round marker, pick up 4 stitches knitwise. 104 (112, 128) sts.

Continue ribbing until hat measures 6 (6, 6.5) inches from bottom of band/block C.

SHAPING CROWN

Round 1 (size 24" only): [[K1, p1] 7 times, k3tog, [p1, k1] 7 times, p1] four times. 120 sts.
All even rounds through Round 26: [K1, p1] around. Begin even rounds after your first odd round.
Round 3: [[K1, p1] 6 times, sssk, [p1, k1] 7 times, p1] four times. 112 sts.
Round 5 (sizes 22" and 24" only): [[K1, p1] 6 times, k3tog, [p1, k1] 6 times, p1] four times. 104 sts.

REMAINING DIRECTIONS ARE FOR ALL SIZES

Round 7: [[K1, p1] 5 times, sssk, [p1, k1] 6 times, p1] four times. 96 sts.
Round 9: [[K1, p1] 5 times, k3tog, [p1, k1] 5 times, p1] four times. 88 sts.
Round 11: [[K1, p1] 4 times, sssk, [p1, k1] 5 times, p1] four times. 80 sts.
Round 13: [[K1, p1] 4 times, k3tog, [p1, k1] 4 times, p1] four times. 72 sts.
Round 15: [[K1, p1] 3 times, sssk, [p1, k1] 4 times, p1] four times. 64 sts.

Round 17: [[K1, p1] 3 times, k3tog, [p1, k1] 3 times, p1] four times. 56 sts.
Round 19: [[K1, p1] 2 times, sssk, [p1, k1] 3 times, p1] four times. 48 sts.
Round 21: [[K1, p1] 2 times, k3tog, [p1, k1] 2 times, p1] four times. 40 sts.
Round 23: [K1, p1, sssk, [p1, k1] 2 times, p1] four times. 32 sts.
Round 25: [K1, p1, k3tog, p1, k1, p1] four times. 24 sts.
Round 27: [Sssk, p1, k1, p1] four times. 16 sts.
Round 28: [K3tog, p1] four times. 8 sts.

FINISHING

Cut the yarn with several inches to work with. With a yarn needle, pull the yarn through all the remaining loops, secure and weave in end. Sew in remaining ends. See Appendix, Entrelac Tips, Terms and Techniques, Sewing in Ends, for tips on how to have a neatly finished edge. Wash and block.

15 ENTRELAC FOLK MITTENS

The rectangles in these mittens are created with ribbed entrelac instead of the traditional stranded knitting. The result is cozy and stretchy.

The style of mittens shown on the cover of Marcia Lewandowski's Folk Mittens have always intrigued me. One day, I decided to recreate the shapes using ribbed entrelac instead of the traditional stranded knitting. The result is cozy and stretchy. Because the number of blocks is integral to the pattern, the different sizes are created by changing the size of the blocks.

These folk mittens are worked in the round, and the top shaping and thumb construction make them a little challenging. If you carefully follow the written directions in conjunction with the diagrams at the top, you'll be back to traditional entrelac quickly. Take the same care with the thumbs. The mittens are worked in k1, p1 ribbed blocks. Size S/M is worked with 7 stitch blocks, and size L/XL with 8 stitch blocks. See Chapter 5, Working Ribbed Blocks. When knitting entrelac in the round, pick up stitches from the point of the block, down towards the valley created with the adjacent block. Halfway through each round, stitches must be shifted around cable, much like using the magic loop method. Unless otherwise noted, instructions are for left and right mittens. Chart A and Chart B refer to the mitered entrelac technique charts on pages 10 and 11.

Sizes
✧ Women's S/M (Women's L/XL or Men's M); shown in Women's size S/M
✧ These mittens are very stretchy, when in doubt, go with the smaller size.

Finished Measurements
✧ Palm circumference: 7 (8)" This measurement is deceptively small; mittens stretch.
✧ Length: 10 (11.5)" This measurement is deceptively long; it's measured point to point.

Materials
✧ Berroco Ultra Alpaca (50% alpaca, 50% wool; 215 yards per 100 gram skein)
  • [MC] Navy #6243; 1 skein, uses approximately 77 (104) yards
  • [CC1] Salt and Pepper #6207; 1 skein, uses approximately 52 (76) yards
  • [CC2] Beet Root #6259; 1 skein, uses approximately 66 (92) yards
✧ 32–40-inch US #6 / 4mm circular needle, or size needed to obtain gauge
✧ Stitch holders

Gauge
30 stitches and 32 rows = 4"/10 cm in k1, p1 ribbing.

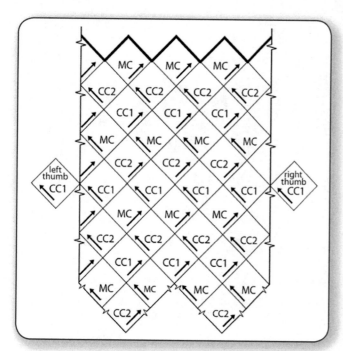

FIGURE 1 Mitten Diagram

HAND INSTRUCTIONS

ROUND 1 With Color CC2, working clockwise (from left to right), follow Chart B on page 11. (Figure 2)

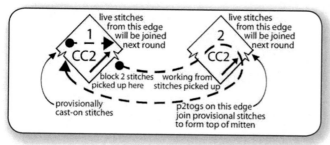

FIGURE 2 Round 1

BLOCK 1 Center-row-setup rectangle.

BLOCK 2 Beginning-of-tier and end-of-round combined rectangle (worked in same color). When finished, block 2 will be back-to-back with block 1. The working stitches will be picked up from the side of block 1, and live stitches will also be joined from block 1, creating the pointed top of the mitten. With each p2tog, the point at the top of the mitten grows. After picking up stitches, and before working row 1, make sure the provisionally cast on stitches are properly mounted on the opposite needle.

ROUND 2 With Color MC, working counterclockwise (from right to left), follow Chart A on page 10. (Figure 3)

BLOCK 1 Beginning-of-round rectangle.

BLOCK 2 End-of-tier rectangle.

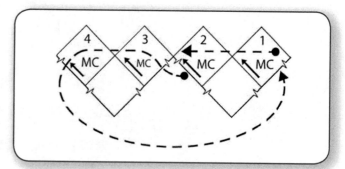

FIGURE 3 Round 2

BLOCK 3 Beginning-of-tier rectangle, stitches picked up from side of block 2 (worked in same color).

BLOCK 4 End-of-round rectangle, joining provisionally cast on stitches from block 1, earlier in round 2.

ROUND 3 With Color CC1, working clockwise (from left to right), follow Chart B on page 11. (Figure 4)

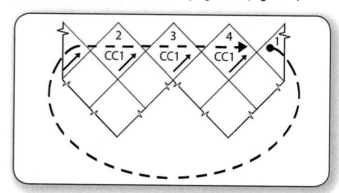

FIGURE 4 Round 3

BLOCKS 1–4 Middle-of-tier rectangles.

ROUND 4 With Color CC2, working counterclockwise, follow Chart A on page 10.

BLOCKS 1–4 Middle-of-tier rectangles.

ROUND 5 With Color MC, working clockwise, follow Chart B on page 11.

BLOCKS 1–4 Middle-of-tier rectangles.

Round 6 is where you create the thumb gusset. Instructions for the left and right mittens are different for rounds 6 and 7. Leave yarn tails several inches longer than usual. It is normal for the transition to the thumb gusset to pull a bit, and you will want to sew in the ends to minimize this.

ROUND 6, LEFT MITTEN ONLY With Color CC1, working counterclockwise, follow Chart A on page 10. (Figure 5)

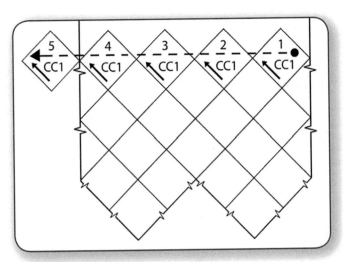

FIGURE 5 Round 6, Left Mitten

BLOCKS 1–4 Middle-of-tier rectangles.
BLOCK 5 Center-row-setup rectangle; this block begins replacing block 1 in round 7. Because these provisionally cast on stitches will be held in reserve until you work the thumb, and not attached later in the same round, use a separate cable or waste yarn, not your working cable to provisionally cast on.

Place stitches from Block 1 onto a stitch holder. Place blocks 1 and 5 back-to-back. Use a safety pin to attach them along the diagonal so that the provisional stitches and the stitches on the holders point in one direction. They will be used later for the thumb. The live stitches from block 5, and the finished edge from block 1 will function as one block for round 7.

ROUND 6, RIGHT MITTEN ONLY With Color CC1, working counterclockwise, follow Chart A. (Figure 6)

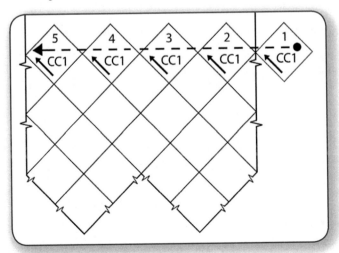

FIGURE 6 Round 6, Right Mitten

BLOCK 1 Center-row-setup rectangle; this block begins replacing block 5 in round 7. Because these

provisionally cast on stitches will be held in reserve until you work the thumb, and not attached later in the same round, use a separate cable or waste yarn, not your working cable to provisionally cast on.
BLOCKS 2–5 Middle-of-tier rectangles.

Place stitches from Block 1 onto a stitch holder. Place blocks 1 and 5 back-to-back. Use a safety pin to attach them along the diagonal so that the provisional stitches and the stitches on the holders point in one direction. They will be used later for the thumb. The live stitches from block 5, and the finished edge from block 1 will function as one block for round 7.

ROUND 7, LEFT MITTEN ONLY With Color CC2, working clockwise, follow Chart B on page 11. The top half of block 5 from round 6 replaces the top half of block 1 from round 6. The top half of block 1 and the bottom half of block 5 are waiting to become thumbs. (Figure 7)

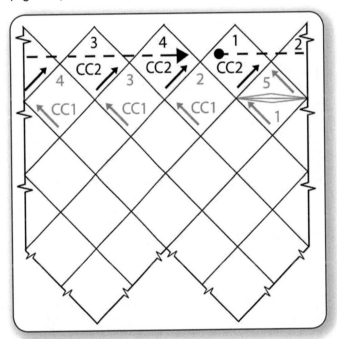

FIGURE 7 Round 7, Left Mitten

BLOCK 1 Middle-of-tier rectangle; stitches picked up from edge of block 2 from round 6 below, and attaching live stitches of block 5 from round 6 below.
BLOCK 2 Middle-of-tier rectangle; stitches picked up from edge of block 5 from round 6 below, and attaching live stitches of block 4 from round 6 below.
BLOCKS 3–4 Middle-of-tier rectangles.

ROUND 7, RIGHT MITTEN ONLY With Color CC2, working clockwise, follow Chart B. The top half of block 1 from round 6 replaces the top half of block 5 from round 6. The top half of block 5 and the bottom half of block 1 are waiting to become thumbs. (Figure 8)

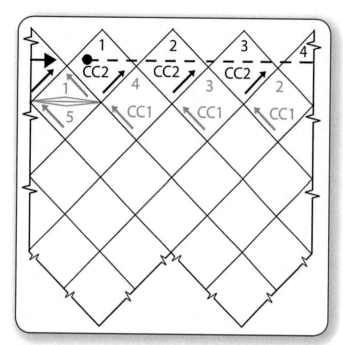

FIGURE 8 *Round 7, Right Mitten*

BLOCK 1 Middle-of-tier rectangle; stitches picked up from edge of block 1 from round 6 below, and attaching live stitches of block 4 from round 6 below.
BLOCKS 2–3 Middle-of-tier rectangles.
BLOCK 4 Middle-of-tier rectangle; stitches picked up from edge of block 2 from round 6 below, and attaching live stitches of block 1 from round 6 below.

Remaining hand instructions are the same for left and right mittens:

ROUND 8 With Color MC, working counterclockwise, follow Chart A on page 10.

BLOCKS 1–4 Middle-of-tier rectangles.

ROUND 9 With Color CC1, working clockwise, follow Chart B on page 11.

BLOCKS 1–4 Middle-of-tier rectangles.

ROUND 10 With Color CC2, working counter-clockwise, follow Chart A on page 10.

BLOCKS 1–4 Middle-of-tier rectangles.

ROUND 11 With Color MC, working clockwise, follow Chart B on page 11.

BLOCKS 1–4 Middle-of-tier rectangles with final row of each block bound-off in pattern. The final stitch of each block will be bound off over first stitch picked up for next block. Sew final stitch of round around original stitch from round to complete the bind-off.

THUMB INSTRUCTIONS

Place stitches from stitch holder and provisional cast-on onto needle. Leave extra cable between the blocks. You may also choose to use three dpns as shown for the purse strap (pages 68 & 69).

ROUND 1 With Color MC, working clockwise, follow Chart B on page 11.

BLOCKS 1–2 Middle-of-tier rectangles.

ROUND 2 With Color CC2, working counterclockwise, follow Chart A on page 10.

BLOCK 1 Middle-of-tier rectangle.
BLOCK 2 Modified middle-of-tier rectangle, attaching or joining stitches on both sides. With RS facing, pick up 7 (8) stitches knitwise, turn.

FOR SIZE S/M:

Odd rows (WS): Sl1p, [k1, p1] to next-to-last stitch, p2tog (last stitch with adjacent stitch from block 1).
Even rows (RS): Sl1k, [p1, k1] to next-to-last stitch, ssk (last stitch of new color with next stitch of old color), turn.

Continue until 13 rows have been worked.

FOR SIZE L/XL:

Odd rows (WS): Sl1k, [p1, k1] to next-to-last stitch, ssk (last stitch with adjacent stitch from block 1).
Even rows (RS): Sl1k, [p1, k1] to next-to-last stitch, ssk (last stitch of new color with next stitch of old color), turn.

Continue until 15 rows have been worked.

For both sizes, finish thumb using one of the following methods:

1. Bind off all stitches; sew top of thumb together.

2. Graft top of thumb together using Kitchner stitch.

Work thumb on second mitten.

FINISHING

Sew in remaining ends, taking special care to close gaps at base of thumb. See Appendix, Entrelac Tips, Terms and Techniques, Sewing in Ends, for tips on how to have a neatly finished edge. Wash and block.

Sizes

Women's XS (S, M, L, XL, XXL);
shown in size XL

Finished Measurements

Collar Length: 26.2 (26.2, 28.6,
28.6, 31, 31)"

Collar Width: 8"

Cape Length: 24 (25, 26, 26.5,
27.5, 28.5)"

Materials

✧ Lion Brand Fisherman's Wool
  (100% wool; 465 yards per
  227 gram skein)
  • [MC] Nature's Brown #126;
    5 skeins, used in cape and
    collar.
  • [CC] Oak Tweed #200; 1
    skein, used in collar only.
  • Yarn is held doubled for
    collar and cape.
✧ 47–60-inch US #11/ 8mm
  circular needle, or size needed
  to obtain gauge
✧ 5 stitch markers
✧ Buckle or sturdy shawl pin

Gauge

13 stitches and 16 rows = 4"/10
cm in stockinette.

16 stitches and 16 rows = 4"/10
cm in k1, p1 ribbing.

16 CAPE

The cape features a mitered entrelac collar in two colors seamlessly attached to a swirling, stockinette cape in one color with a seed stitch border. The project is worked from the top down, working the collar first, and then the cape.

The cape collar is worked with 5 stitch ribbed blocks with yarn doubled. See Chapter 5, Working Ribbed Blocks. Because of the length, the top and right side tiers are worked first. The bottom and left side tiers are worked afterwards. Chart A and Chart B refer to the mitered entrelac technique charts on pages 10 and 1. (Figure 1) To complete the collar, you will fill in the triangular openings between the entrelac points. These will not be standard entrelac triangles worked on the diagonal, but will be worked straight back and forth.

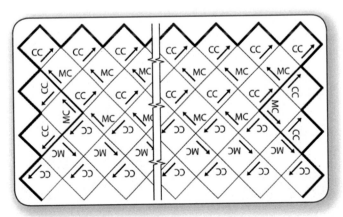

FIGURE 1 Cape Collar Diagram

COLLAR INSTRUCTIONS

ROUND 1 With Color MC, working counterclockwise (from right to left), follow Chart A on page 10. (Figure 2)

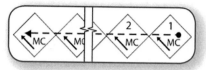

FIGURE 2 Collar Round 1

BLOCKS 1–8 (8, 9, 9, 10, 10) Center-row-setup rectangles; only provisionally cast on the stitches for one block at a time.

ROUND 2 (FIRST HALF) With Colors CC and MC, working clockwise (from left to right), follow Chart B on page 11. (Figure 3)

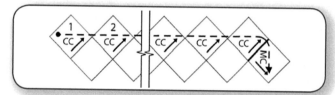

FIGURE 3 Round 2 (First Half)

TOP TIER, COLOR CC
BLOCK 1 Beginning-of-round rectangle.
BLOCKS 2–8 (8, 9, 9, 10, 10) Middle-of-tier rectangles.
BLOCK 9 (9, 10, 10, 11, 11) End-of-tier rectangle.

RIGHT SIDE, COLOR MC
BLOCK 10 (10, 11, 11, 12, 12) Beginning- and end-of-tier rectangle.

ROUND 3 (FIRST HALF) With Colors CC and MC, working counterclockwise, follow Chart A on page 10. (Figure 4)

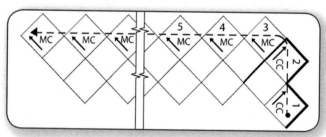

FIGURE 4 Round 3 (First Half)

RIGHT SIDE TIER, COLOR CC
BLOCK 1 Beginning-of-round rectangle with bind-off.
BLOCK 2 End-of-tier rectangle with bind-off.

TOP TIER, COLOR MC
BLOCK 3 Beginning-of-tier rectangle.

BLOCKS 4–11 (11, 12, 12, 13, 13) Middle-of-tier rectangles.
BLOCK 12 (12, 13, 13, 14, 14) End-of-tier rectangle.

ROUND 4 (FIRST HALF) With Color CC, working clockwise, follow Chart B on page 11.

TOP TIER, COLOR CC
BLOCK 1 Cast-on rectangle with bind-off.
BLOCKS 2–10 (10, 11, 11, 12, 12) Middle-of-tier rectangles with bind-off.
BLOCK 11 (11, 12, 12, 13, 13) End-of-tier rectangle with bind-off.

ROUND 2 (SECOND HALF) With Colors CC and MC, working clockwise (from left to right), follow Chart B on page 11. (Figure 5)

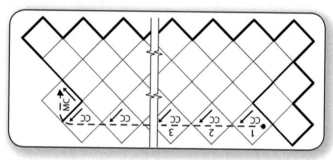

FIGURE 5 Round 2 (Second Half)

BOTTOM TIER, COLOR CC
BLOCK 1 Beginning-of-tier rectangle.
BLOCKS 2–8 (8, 9, 9, 10, 10) Middle-of-tier rectangles. Note that for these blocks, you will be picking up stitches from the bottom to the top of the entrelac block below; not top to bottom as normal.
BLOCK 9 (9, 10, 10, 11, 11) End-of-tier rectangle.

LEFT SIDE TIER, COLOR MC
BLOCK 10 (10, 11, 11, 12, 12) Beginning-of-tier and end-of-round combined rectangle.

ROUND 3 (SECOND HALF) With Colors CC and MC, working counterclockwise, follow Chart A on page 10. (Figure 6)

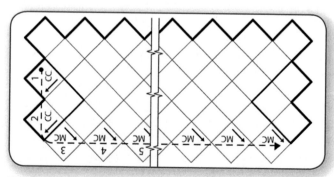

FIGURE 6 Round 3 (Second Half)

LEFT SIDE TIER, COLOR CC
BLOCK 1 Beginning-of-tier rectangle with bind-off.
BLOCK 2 End-of-tier rectangle with bind-off.

BOTTOM TIER, COLOR MC
BLOCK 3 Beginning-of-tier rectangle.
BLOCKS 4–11 (11, 12, 12, 13, 13) Middle-of-tier rectangles.
BLOCK 12 (12, 13, 13, 14, 14) End-of-round rectangle.

ROUND 4 (SECOND HALF) With Color CC, working clockwise, follow Chart B on page 11.

BOTTOM, COLOR CC
BLOCK 1 Cast-on rectangle; no bind-off, these stitches are left on needle to work cape.
BLOCKS 2–10 (10, 11, 11, 12, 12) Middle-of-tier rectangles; no bind-off.
BLOCK 11 (11, 12, 12 13, 13) End-of-tier rectangle with bind-off, these stitches will not be used for cape.

FILLING IN THE BOTTOM OF THE COLLAR

To complete the collar, you will fill in the triangular openings between the entrelac points with seed stitch. Unlike standard entrelac triangles worked on the diagonal, these will be worked straight back and forth. Like standard entrelac triangles, each triangle will begin with picking up stitches along the edge of a block below, and each triangle will be completed before beginning the next triangle.

BLOCK 1 First fill-in triangle (Figure 7)

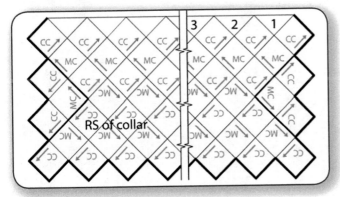

FIGURE 7 Filling in Collar

With RS facing, and a double strand of MC, pick up 6 stitches knitwise along edge of last block of collar worked (pick up the "extra" stitch along the 5-stitch block in the "valley" between two blocks). Since you are working along the bottom of the collar, this will be on the right edge of your work. Turn. Your first row will work only the last two stitches picked up.

Row 1 (WS): Sl1p, k1, turn (4 picked-up stitches unworked).

Row 2 (RS): Sl1k, ssk (last stitch of new color with next stitch of old color), turn.
Row 3: Sl1p, k1, purl next picked up stitch, turn (3 picked-up stitches unworked).
Row 4: Sl1p, k1, ssk (last stitch of new color with next stitch of old color), turn.
Row 5: Sl1p, k1, p1, knit next picked up stitch, turn (2 picked-up stitches unworked).
Row 6: Sl1k, p1, k1, ssk (last stitch of new color with next stitch of old color), turn.
Row 7: Sl1p, k1, p1, k1, purl next picked up stitch, turn (1 picked-up stitch unworked).
Row 8: Sl1p, k1, p1, k1, ssk (last stitch of new color with next stitch of old color), turn.
Row 9: Sl1p, k1, p1, k1, p1, knit final picked up stitch, turn.
Row 10: Sl1k, p1, k1, p1, k1, ssk (last stitch of new color with next stitch of old color), turn.

First fill-in triangle completed.

BLOCKS 2–10 (10, 11, 11, 12, 12) Remaining fill-in triangles:

With RS facing, and MC, pick up 6 stitches knitwise along edge block below; turn.

Rows 1–8: same as first fill-in triangle
Row 9: Sl1p, k1, p1, k1, p1, knit final picked up stitch, w&t (last stitch from previous fill-in triangle).
Row 10: K1, p1, k1, p1, k1, ssk (last stitch of new color with next stitch of old color), turn.

After completing the final triangle you should have 60 (60, 66, 66, 72, 72) stitches, six stitches from each fill-in triangle.

CAPE INSTRUCTIONS

When the collar folds down, both the front of the collar and the front of the cape should be facing out. To do this, the RS of the cape will be worked on the WS of the collar. The neck band will continue in seed stitch. The rest of the cape will be knit in stockinette with seed stitch borders.

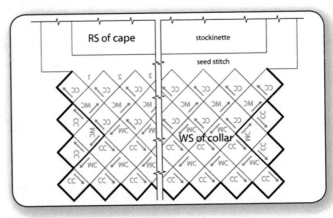

FIGURE 8 Collar Transition to Cape

Row 1 (WS of cape, RS of collar): Using doubled strand of MC from filling-in, and a cabled cast-on, cast on 6 stitches; 66 (66, 72, 72, 78, 78) stitches.

Row 2 (RS of cape, WS of collar): Sl1p, [k1, p1] across to last stitch, k1, using a cabled cast-on, cast on 6 stitches; 72 (72, 78, 78, 84, 84) stitches.

Rows 3, 5: Sl1k, [p1, k1] across to last stitch, p1.

Rows 4, 6: Sl1p, [k1, p1] across to last stitch, k1.

In row 7, you will be placing the five markers where you will work increases on certain rows.

Row 7 (sizes XS/S): Sl1k, [p1, k1] 7 times, p1, PM, {[k1, p1] 5 times, PM} 4 times, [k1, p1] 8 times (omitting seed stitch borders, 10 stitches between markers).

Row 7 (sizes M/ L): Sl1k, [p1, k1] 8 times, PM, {[p1, k1] 5 times, p1, PM, [k1, p1] 5 times, k1, PM]} 2 times, [p1, k1] 8 times, p1 (omitting seed stitch borders, 11 stitches between markers).

Row 7 (sizes XL/XXL): Sl1k, [p1, k1] 8 times, p1, PM, {[k1, p1] 6 times, PM} 4 times, [k1, p1] 9 times (omitting seed stitch borders, 12 stitches between markers).

Row 8: (increase row): Sl1p, [k1, p1] two times, [knit to marker, m1, slip marker, m1] five times, knit across to last 6 stitches, [p1, k1] three times (10 stitch increase).

Row 9 and all odd rows: Sl1k, [p1, k1] two times, slipping markers as you work, purl across to last 6 stitches, [k1, p1] three times.

Row 10: Sl1p, [k1, p1] two times, slipping markers as you work, knit across to last 6 stitches, [p1, k1] three times.

Repeat rows 8–11, ending with a row 8, until a length of 22.5 (23.5, 24.5, 25, 26, 27)", or an inch and a half shorter than desired length.

BOTTOM BORDER

Rows 1, 3, 5, 7: Sl1k, [p1, k1] across to last stitch, p1.

Rows 2, 4, 6: Sl1p, [k1, p1] across to last stitch, k1.

Row 8: Continuing seed stitch pattern from even rows, bind off all stitches.

FINISHING

Sew in remaining ends. If desired, attach buckle closure at neck edge. See Appendix, Entrelac Tips, Terms and Techniques, Sewing in Ends, for tips on how to have a neatly finished edge. Wash and block.

Sizes

Doll, Infants, Children: 16–18" doll (Child's 3–9 mos., 12 mos.–2T, 4–6 yrs., 8–10 yrs.)

Finished Measurements

Shoulder Width: 5.5 (7, 8.5, 10, 11.5)"

Length at center front: 7 (13, 16, 19, 22)"

Materials

✧ Cascade 220 Superwash (100% wool; 220 yards per 100 gram skein)
  • [Color A] Dark Aqua #849; 1(1, 1, 1, 2) skein(s), uses approximately 60 (95, 135, 180, 235) yards
  • [Color B] Oceanside #826; 1(1, 1, 2, 2) skein(s), uses approximately 90 (140, 200, 270, 350) yards
  • [Color C] Wasabi #887; 1 skein, uses approximately 45 (70, 100, 135, 180) yards
✧ 47–60-inch US #7 / 4.5mm circular needle, or size needed to obtain gauge

Gauge

20 stitches and 30 rows = 4"/10 cm in stockinette stitch.

17 PONCHO

This poncho is a no buttons, easy, no fuss way to keep your favorite child warm. Just pick some favorite colors, and before you know it, you'll have a comfortable, happy child.

This poncho is knit from the top down using mitered entrelac, but there are only two "corners," one in the front, and one in the back. The different sizes are worked by changing the size of each entrelac block. All blocks are stockinette. For size 16-18" doll (Child's 3-9 mos., 12 mos.–2T, 4–6 yrs., 8–10 yrs.), work 4– (5–, 6–, 7–, 8–) stitch blocks. (Figure 1) Chart A and Chart

B refer to the mitered entrelac technique charts on pages 10 and 11. If you are not confident which size to knit, while knitting the first few rounds, do not break yarn; just make sure you leave enough yarn for two tails and connect the next place each color is used. That way if you unravel and start over, you aren't left with many pieces of yarn in awkward lengths.

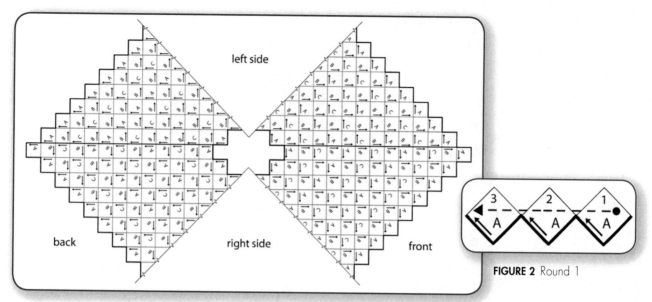

FIGURE 1 Poncho Diagram

FIGURE 2 Round 1

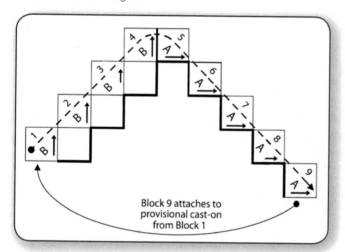

Block 9 attaches to
provisional cast-on
from Block 1

FIGURE 3 Round 2

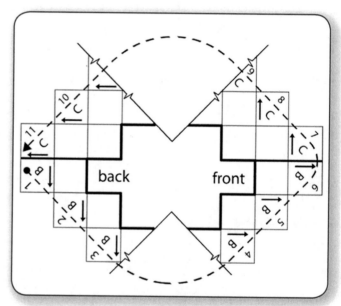

FIGURE 4 Round 3

ROUND 1 Neck edge, working counterclockwise (from right to left), with Color A, follow Chart A on page 10. (Figure 2)

LEFT SIDE TIER, COLOR A

BLOCKS 1–3 Using a knitted cast-on, cast on 4 (5, 6, 7, 8) stitches, then work as end-of-tier rectangle.

ROUND 2 With Colors B and A, working clockwise (from left to right), follow Chart B on page 11. (Figure 3)

LEFT SIDE TIER, COLOR B

BLOCK 1 Beginning-of-round rectangle.
BLOCKS 2–3 Middle-of-tier rectangles.
BLOCK 4 End-of-tier rectangle.

RIGHT SIDE TIER, COLOR A

BLOCK 5 Beginning- and end-of-tier rectangle.
BLOCKS 6–8 Using a knitted cast-on, cast on 4 (5, 6, 7, 8) stitches, then work as end-of-tier rectangle.

BLOCK 9 Cast on stitches for rectangle as with other cast-on rectangles, then, being careful not to twist, work as an end-of-round rectangle joining or attaching stitches provisionally cast on at beginning of round.

ROUND 3 With Colors B and C, working counterclockwise, follow Chart A on page 10. (Figure 4)

RIGHT SIDE TIER, COLOR B

BLOCK 1 Beginning-of-round rectangle.
BLOCKS 2–5 Middle-of-tier rectangles.
BLOCK 6 End-of-tier rectangle.

LEFT SIDE TIER, COLOR C

BLOCK 7 Beginning-of-round rectangle.
BLOCKS 8–10 Middle-of-tier rectangles.
BLOCK 11 End-of-round rectangle.

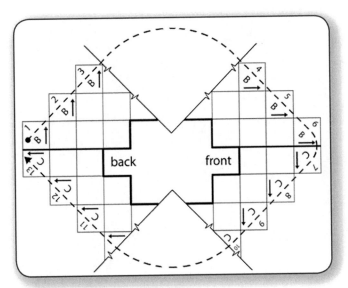

FIGURE 5 Round 4

ROUND 4 With Colors B and C, working clockwise, follow Chart B on page 11. (Figure 5)

LEFT SIDE TIER, COLOR C
BLOCK 1 Beginning-of-round rectangle.
BLOCKS 2–5 Middle-of-tier rectangles.
BLOCK 6 End-of-tier rectangle.

RIGHT SIDE TIER, COLOR B
BLOCK 7 Beginning-of-tier rectangle.
BLOCKS 8–12 Middle-of-tier rectangles.
BLOCK 13 End-of-round rectangle.

ROUND 5 With Colors B and A, working counter-clockwise, follow Chart A on page 10.

RIGHT SIDE TIER, COLOR B
BLOCK 1 Beginning-of-round rectangle.
BLOCKS 2–7 Middle-of-tier rectangles.
BLOCK 8 End-of-tier rectangle.

LEFT SIDE TIER, COLOR A
BLOCK 9 Beginning-of-tier rectangle.
BLOCKS 10–14 Middle-of-tier rectangles.
BLOCK 15 End-of-round rectangle.

ROUND 6 With Colors B and A, working clockwise, follow Chart B on page 11.

LEFT SIDE TIER, COLOR B
BLOCK 1 Beginning-of-round rectangle.
BLOCKS 2–7 Middle-of-tier rectangles.
BLOCK 8 End-of-tier rectangle.

RIGHT SIDE TIER, COLOR A
BLOCK 9 Beginning-of-tier rectangle.
BLOCKS 10–17 Middle-of-tier rectangles.

ROUND 7 With Colors B and C, working counter-clockwise, follow Chart A on page 10.

RIGHT SIDE TIER, COLOR B
BLOCK 1 Beginning-of-round rectangle.
BLOCKS 2–9 Middle-of-tier rectangles.
BLOCK 10 End-of-tier rectangle.

LEFT SIDE TIER, COLOR C
BLOCK 11 Beginning-of-tier rectangle.
BLOCKS 12–18 Middle-of-tier rectangles.
BLOCK 19 End-of-round rectangle.

ROUND 8 With Colors B and C, working clockwise, follow Chart B on page 11.

LEFT SIDE TIER, COLOR B
BLOCK 1 Beginning-of-round rectangle.
BLOCKS 2–9 Middle-of-tier rectangles.
BLOCK 10 End-of-tier rectangle.

RIGHT SIDE TIER, COLOR C
BLOCK 11 Beginning-of-tier rectangle.
BLOCKS 12–20 Middle-of-tier rectangles.
BLOCK 21 End-of-round rectangle.

ROUND 9 With Colors B and A, working counter-clockwise, follow Chart A on page 10.

RIGHT SIDE TIER, COLOR B
BLOCK 1 Beginning-of-round rectangle.
BLOCKS 2–11 Middle-of-tier rectangles.
BLOCK 12 End-of-tier rectangle.

LEFT SIDE TIER, COLOR A
BLOCK 13 Beginning-of-tier rectangle (for doll size only, with bind-off).
BLOCKS 14–22 Middle-of-tier rectangles. (for doll size only, with bind-off).
BLOCK 23 End-of-round rectangle (for doll size only, with bind-off).

ROUND 10 With Colors B and A, working clockwise, follow Chart B on page 11.

LEFT SIDE TIER, COLOR B
BLOCK 1 Beginning-of-round rectangle (for doll size only, not worked).
BLOCKS 2–11 Middle-of-tier rectangles (for doll size only, not worked).
BLOCK 12 End-of-tier rectangle (for doll size only, not worked).

RIGHT SIDE TIER, COLOR A
BLOCK 13 Beginning-of-tier rectangle (for doll size only, cast-on-rectangle with bind-off).
BLOCKS 14–24 Middle-of-tier rectangles (for doll size only, bind-off).
BLOCK 25 End-of-round rectangle (for doll size only, end-of-tier rectangle with bind-off).

Doll poncho finished.

ROUND 11 With Colors B and C, working counter-clockwise, follow Chart A on page 10.

RIGHT SIDE TIER, COLOR B
BLOCK 1 Beginning-of-round rectangle.
BLOCKS 2–13 Middle-of-tier rectangles.
BLOCK 14 End-of-tier rectangle.

LEFT SIDE TIER, COLOR C
BLOCK 15 Beginning-of-tier rectangle.
BLOCKS 16–26 Middle-of-tier rectangles.
BLOCK 27 End-of-round rectangle.

ROUND 12 With Colors B and C, working clockwise, follow Chart B on page 11.

LEFT SIDE TIER, COLOR B
BLOCK 1 Beginning-of-round rectangle.
BLOCKS 2–13 Middle-of-tier rectangles.
BLOCK 14 End-of-tier rectangle.

RIGHT SIDE TIER, COLOR C
BLOCK 15 Beginning-of-tier rectangle.
BLOCKS 16–28 Middle-of-tier rectangles.
BLOCK 29 End-of-round rectangle.

ROUND 13 With Colors B and A, working counter-clockwise, follow Chart A on page 10.

RIGHT SIDE TIER, COLOR B
BLOCK 1 Beginning-of-round rectangle.
BLOCKS 2–15 Middle-of-tier rectangles.
BLOCK 16 End-of-tier rectangle.

LEFT SIDE TIER, COLOR A
BLOCK 17 Beginning-of-tier rectangle with bind-off.
BLOCKS 18–30 Middle-of-tier rectangles with bind-off.
BLOCK 31 End-of-round rectangle with bind-off.

ROUND 14 With Color A, working clockwise, follow Chart B on page 11.

RIGHT SIDE TIER, COLOR A
BLOCK 1 Cast-on rectangle with bind-off.
BLOCKS 2–16 Middle-of-tier rectangles with bind-off.
BLOCK 17 End-of-tier rectangle with bind-off.

FINISHING

Sew in ends. See Appendix, Entrelac Tips, Terms and Techniques, Sewing in Ends, for tips on how to have a neatly finished edge. Wash and block.

Finished Measurements

6" x 6" purse flap, 9.25" x 9.25" purse body, 28" strap

Materials

✧ KnitPicks Swish Worsted (100% superwash merino wool; 110 yards per 50 gram skein)
  • [MC] Cobblestone Heather; 3 skeins
  • [CC1] Dove Heather; 1 skein
✧ KnitPicks Swish Tonal (100% superwash merino wool; 220 yards per 100 gram skein)
  • [CC2] Thunderhead Tonal; 1 skein
✧ 32–40-inch US #10.5 / 6.5mm circular needle, or size needed to obtain gauge
✧ 3 dp US #7 / 4.5mm circular needles, or size needed to obtain gauge. May use other needle type to knit cord if preferred.
✧ Button
✧ 2 stitch markers

Gauge

18 stitches and 20 rows = 4"/10 cm in with yarn doubled in stockinette stitch. Gauge is not critical in this pattern, but a different gauge will affect yardage and size of finished item.

This purse features a mitered entrelac flap, and introduces entrelac cord, e-cord. The body is knit onto the flap and straps, and incorporates the flap using entrelac-style joining.

The purse flap and body are worked using two strands of yarn (doubled), the flap with 5 stitch stockinette blocks. The purse strap is worked using a single strand of yarn with 5 stitch stockinette blocks. Chart A and Chart B refer to the mitered entrelac technique charts on pages 10 and 11.

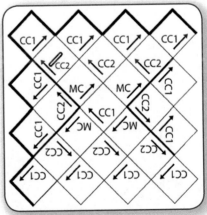

FIGURE 1 Purse Flap Diagram

FLAP INSTRUCTIONS

Flap is knit with 5 stitch, stockinette rectangles, with yarn doubled, on smaller needles.

ROUND 1 Center row, working counterclockwise (from right to left), with Color CC1, follow Chart A on page 10. (Figure 2)
BLOCK 1 Center-row-setup rectangle.

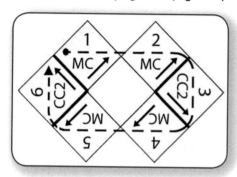

FIGURE 2 Round 1

ROUND 2 With Colors MC and CC2, working clockwise (from left to right), follow Chart B on page 11. (Figure 3)

FIGURE 3 Round 2

TOP TIER, COLOR MC
BLOCK 1 Beginning-of-round rectangle.
BLOCK 2 End-of-tier rectangle.

RIGHT SIDE TIER, COLOR CC2
BLOCK 3 Beginning- and end-of-tier rectangle.

BOTTOM TIER, COLOR MC
BLOCK 4 Beginning-of-tier rectangle.
BLOCK 5 End-of-tier rectangle. Note that for this block, you will be picking up stitches from the bottom to the top of the entrelac block below; not top to bottom as normal.

LEFT SIDE TIER, COLOR CC2
BLOCK 6 Beginning-of-tier and end-of-round combined rectangle.

ROUND 3 With Colors CC1 and CC2, working counterclockwise, follow Chart A on page 10. (Figure 4)

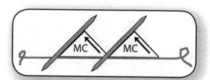

FIGURE 4 Round 3

LEFT SIDE TIER, COLOR CC1
BLOCK 1 Beginning-of-round rectangle with bind-off.
BLOCK 2 End-of-tier rectangle with bind-off.

BOTTOM TIER, COLOR CC2
BLOCK 3 Beginning-of-tier rectangle.
BLOCK 4 Middle-of-tier rectangle.
BLOCK 5 End-of-tier rectangle.

RIGHT SIDE TIER, COLOR CC1
BLOCK 6 Beginning-of-tier rectangle; no bind-off, these stitches are left on needle to be worked into purse body.
BLOCK 7 End-of-tier rectangle, no bind-off.

TOP TIER, COLOR CC2
BLOCK 8 Beginning-of-tier rectangle.
BLOCK 9 Middle-of-tier rectangle.
BLOCK 10 End-of-round rectangle with buttonhole:

Row 4: Sl1k, k1, bind off 2 stitches, ssk last stitch of new color with next stitch of old color, turn.
Row 5: Sl1p, cast on 2, p2, turn.

ROUND 4 With Color CC1, working clockwise, follow Chart B on page 11.

TOP TIER, COLOR CC1
BLOCK 1 Cast-on rectangle with bind-off.
BLOCKS 2–3 Middle-of-tier rectangles with bind-off.
BLOCK 4 End-of-tier rectangle with bind-off.

BOTTOM TIER, COLOR CC1
BLOCK 5 Beginning-of-round rectangle; no bind-off, these stitches are left on needle to be worked into purse body.
BLOCKS 6–7 Middle-of-tier rectangles, no bind-off.
BLOCK 8 End-of-tier rectangle with bind-off; these stitches will not be worked into purse body.

STRAP INSTRUCTIONS—E-CORD

E-cord, or entrelac cord is entrelac in the round worked with only two blocks in each round. Working E-cord is not as easy or fast as I-cord, but it does make a very sturdy strap. This strap is knit in 5 stitch, stockinette blocks with a single strand of yarn on smaller (dpn) needles. The strap begins and ends with triangles, and all the other blocks are middle-of-tier rectangles.

ROUND 1 With Color MC, working counterclockwise.
BLOCKS 1–2 Base triangles. (Figure 5)

FIGURE 5 Strap, Beginning Round 1

Using one dpn, provisionally cast on 10 stitches. Because these stitches will be held in reserve until you complete the strap, and not attached later in the same round, use waste yarn, not your working needle to cast on.

First base triangle is worked on second 5 provisionally cast on stitches.

Row 1 (RS): K2, turn.
Row 2 (WS): Sl1p, p1, turn.
Row 3: Sl1k, k2, turn.
Row 4: Sl1p, p2, turn.
Row 5: Sl1k, k3, turn.
Row 6: Sl1p, p3, turn.
Row 7: Sl1k, k4, turn.
Row 8: Sl1p, p4, turn.
Row 9: Sl1k, k4, do not turn.

Second base triangle is worked on 5 remaining provisionally cast on stitches. Leave a dpn in first triangle, and work second triangle with the other two dpns.

ROUND 2 With Color CC1, working clockwise (from left to right), follow Chart B on page 11. (Figure 6)

BLOCK 1 Using third dpn, pick up stitches from top of triangle 2 to base of triangle. Work a middle-of-tier rectangle. (Figure 7)

FIGURE 6 Strap, Beginning Round 2

BLOCK 2 Using an empty dpn, pick up stitches from top of triangle 1 to base of triangle. Being careful not to twist strap, fold work so that two MC triangles are back to back.

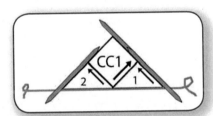

FIGURE 7 Strap, First Block of Round 2

Work a middle-of-tier rectangle with stitches picked up from triangle 1 and attaching or joining live stitches from triangle 2.

ROUND 3 With Color CC2, working counterclockwise, follow Chart A on page 10.

BLOCKS 1–2 Middle-of-tier rectangles.

ROUND 4 With Color MC, working clockwise, follow Chart B on page 11.

BLOCKS 1–2 Middle-of-tier rectangles.

ROUND 5 With Color CC1, working counterclockwise, follow Chart A on page 10.

BLOCKS 1–2 Middle-of-tier rectangles.

ROUND 6 With Color CC2, working clockwise, follow Chart B on page 11.

BLOCKS 1–2 Middle-of-tier rectangles.

ROUND 7 With Color MC, working counterclockwise, follow Chart A on page 10.

BLOCKS 1–2 Middle-of-tier rectangles.

ROUND 8 With Color CC1, working clockwise, follow Chart B on page 11.

BLOCKS 1–2 Middle-of-tier rectangles.

ROUNDS 9–42 repeat rounds 3-8, ending with a round 6.

ROUND 43 With Color MC, working counterclockwise.

BLOCKS 1–2 Top triangles.

With RS facing, pick up 5 stitches knitwise along edge of block below; turn.

Row 1 (WS): Sl1p, p4, turn.
Rows 2, 4, 6, 8 (RS): Sl1k, knit to next-to-last stitch, ssk (last stitch of new color with next stitch of old color), turn.
Row 3: Sl1p, p3, turn.
Row 5: Sl1p, p2, turn.
Row 7: Sl1p, p1, turn.
Row 9: Sl1p, turn.
Row 10: SSK (last stitch of new color with next stitch of old color), do not turn.

BODY OF PURSE INSTRUCTIONS (FIGURES 8 & 9)

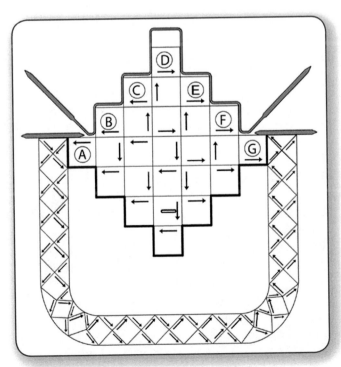

FIGURE 8 Joining Flap and Straps to Purse Body

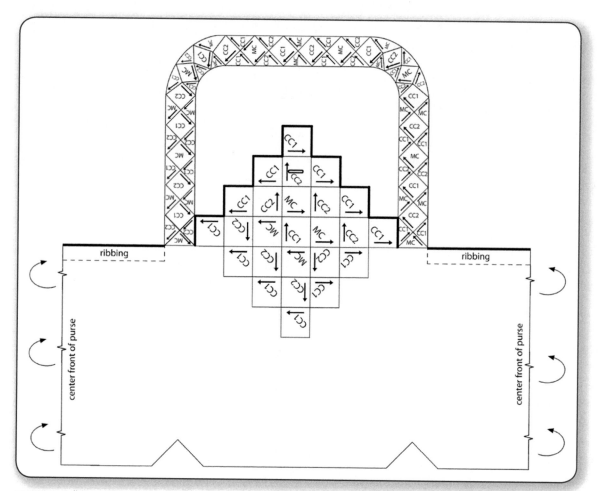

FIGURE 9 Full Purse Diagram

Row 1 (RS): Using two strands of MC and larger needles, pick up 5 stitches along top of block A (note that along this edge, you will be picking up stitches backwards); knit 5 stitches from strap (each stitch has 1 stitch from front of strap, and 1 stitch from back of strap). Cast on 35 stitches, a ribbed cable cast-on beginning with a purl stitch is recommended. Being careful not to twist, knit 5 stitches from other end of handle, combing stitches as on other end of strap; pick up 5 stitches along top edge of block G. (55 horizontal stitches total, doesn't include vertical stitches from purse flap waiting to be attached.)

Rows 2, 4, 6, 8 (WS): Sl1p, p9, (k1, p1) for 35 stitches, p9, p2tog with first stitch from side of block B.

Rows 3, 5, 7, 9: Sl1k, k9, (p1, k1) for 35 stitches, k9, ssk with first stitch from side of block F.

Row 10: Sl1p, purl until last stitch, p2tog last stitch of row with last stitch from side of block B, pick up 5 stitches along top edge of block B. 60 sts.

Row 11: Sl1k, knit until last stitch, ssk last stitch of row with last stitch from side of block F, pick up 5 stitches along top edge of block F. 65 sts.

Rows 12, 14, 16, 18: Sl1p, purl until last stitch, p2tog last stitch of row with next stitch from side of block C.

Rows 13, 15, 17, 19: Sl1k , knit until last stitch, ssk last stitch of row with next stitch from side of block E.

Row 20: Sl1p, purl until last stitch, p2tog last stitch of row with last stitch from side of block C, pick up 5 stitches along top edge of block C. 70 sts. The provisionally cast on stitches from Block D need to be mounted properly for attaching.

Row 21: Sl1k, knit until last stitch, ssk last stitch of row with last stitch from side of block E, pick up 5 stitches along top edge of block E. 75 sts.

Rows 22, 24, 26, 28: Sl1p, purl until last stitch, p2tog last stitch of row with next stitch from side of block D.

Rows 23, 25, 27, 29: Sl1k, knit until last stitch, ssk last stitch of row with next stitch from side of block D.

Row 30: Sl1p, purl until last stitch, p2tog last stitch of row with last stitch from side of block D, pick up 5 stitches along top edge of block C, place round marker. 80 sts.

Row 31: Sl1k, knit all.

You will now begin knitting in the round.

Rounds 32–52 (or until purse measures 8 inches): Knit all.
Round 53: Insert markers at each side of purse. Knit until 2 stitches before marker, k2tog, ssk, knit until 2

stitches before marker, k2tog, ssk, knit rest of round. 76 sts.

Round 54: Knit all.

Round 55: Insert markers at each side of purse. Knit until 2 stitches before marker, k2tog, ssk, knit until 2 stitches before marker, k2tog, ssk, knit rest of round. 72 sts.

Round 56: Knit all.

Round 57: Insert markers at each side of purse. Knit until 2 stitches before marker, k2tog, ssk, knit until 2 stitches before marker, k2tog, ssk, knit rest of round. 68 sts.

Round 58: Knit all.

Round 59: Insert markers at each side of purse. Knit until 2 stitches before marker, k2tog, ssk, knit until 2 stitches before marker, k2tog, ssk, knit rest of round. 64 sts.

Round 60: Knit all.

Round 61: Insert markers at each side of purse. Knit until 2 stitches before marker, k2tog, ssk, knit until 2 stitches before marker, k2tog, ssk, knit rest of round. 60 sts.

Round 62: Knit all, then knit to next side marker. Bottom of purse: Finish bottom of purse using one of the following methods:

1. Bind off all stitches; sew bottom of purse together.

2. Bind off bottom of purse using 3-needle bind-off.

3. Graft bottom of purse together using Kitchner stitch.

FINISHING

Sew button to front of purse under buttonhole. Sew in ends. See Appendix, Entrelac Tips, Terms and Techniques, Sewing in Ends, for tips on how to have a neatly finished edge. Wash and block.

Sizes

Doll, Infants, Children: 16-18"
doll (Child's 3-6 mos., 9-12 mos.,
18mos.-2T, 4-6 yrs., 8-10 yrs.)

Finished Measurements

Chest: 13 (17, 21, 25, 29, 33)"
Designed with generous ease for
a comfortable fit.

Materials – royal colors

◇ Cascade 220 Superwash
  (100% wool; 220 yards per
  100 gram skein)
  • [Color A] Blue Velvet #813;
    1 skein, uses approximately
    45 (70, 95, 130, 170, 215)
    yards
  • [Color B] Christmas Green
    #864; 1 skein, uses approxi-
    mately 40 (60, 90, 120, 160,
    200) yards
  • [Color C] Lemon #820; 1
    skein, uses approximately
    45 (70, 95, 130, 170, 215)
    yards
  • [Color D] Purple Hyacinth
    #1986; 1 skein, uses approxi-
    mately 45 (70, 95, 130, 170,
    215) yards
  • [Color E] Ruby #893; 1 skein,
    uses approximately 35 (55,
    80, 105, 140, 175) yards

19 RAGLAN SWEATER FOR CHILDREN AND BABIES

*Any child or baby wearing this Mitered Entrelac sweater will be too cute
for words. Knit it in royal colors, bright pastels, or use your imagination.
Personalize your choice with a Peter Pan collar or jester's points.*

This sweater is knit from the top down in a raglan
entrelac pattern. It uses the intrinsic entrelac shape
to create the edges. The yoke is knit using the
mitered entrelac technique. Because it is a cardigan, with
a right and left front, each yoke round will have five tiers.
The yoke is completed in just four rounds. After that, the
body and arms of the sweater use only traditional entrelac
blocks. Because the number of blocks is integral to the
design of the pattern, the different sizes are worked by
changing the size of each entrelac block. All blocks are
stockinette. For size 16–18" doll (Child's 3–6 mos., 9–12

mos., 18mos.–2T, 4–6 yrs., 8–10 yrs.), work 4– (5–,
6–, 7–, 8–, 9–) stitch blocks. Chart A and Chart B refer
to the mitered entrelac technique charts on pages 10
and 11. Directions for the triangle blocks will be given
where they occur. If you are not confident which size to
knit, while knitting yoke, do not break yarn; just make
sure you leave enough yarn for two tails and connect
the next place each color is used. That way if you
unravel and start over, you aren't left with many pieces
of yarn in awkward lengths. (Figure 1)

YOKE INSTRUCTIONS

ROUND 1 With Colors A and B, working counter-clockwise (from right to left), follow Chart A on page 10. (Figure 2)

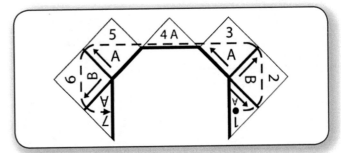

FIGURE 2 Round 1

Note: In Round 1, because there are no existing blocks to attach, all rectangles are end-of-tier.

LEFT FRONT TIER, COLOR A
BLOCK 1 Left front triangle.
Row 1 (RS): Cast on 1, turn.
Row 2 (WS): Pf&b, turn. 2 sts.
Row 3: Sl1k, k1, turn.
Row 4: Sl1p, pf&b, turn. 3 sts.
Row 5: Sl1k, k2, turn.
Row 6: Sl1p, purl across to last stitch, pf&b, turn. 1 add'l st.
Row 7: Sl1k, knit across, turn.

Repeat rows 6 and 7 until you have 4 (5, 6, 7, 8, 9) stitches.

Triangle complete.

LEFT SLEEVE TIER, COLOR B
BLOCK 2 Beginning- and end-of-tier rectangle.

BACK TIER, COLOR A
BLOCK 3 Beginning- and end-of-tier rectangle.
BLOCK 4 Base triangle.

Cast on 1.

Row 1 (WS): P1, turn.
Row 2 (RS): Kf&b, turn. 2 sts.
Row 3: Sl1p, p1, turn.
Row 4: Sl1k, kf&b, turn. 3 sts.
Row 5: Sl1p, p2, turn.
Row 6: Sl1k, knit across to last stitch, kf&b, turn. 1 add'l st.
Row 7: Sl1p, purl across, turn.

Repeat rows 6 and 7 until you have 4 (5, 6, 7, 8, 9) stitches.

Row 8 (10, 12, 14, 16, 18): Sl1k, knit across.
Triangle complete.

Materials (bright pastels)
✧ Ella Rae Classic Solids (100% wool; 219 yards per 100 gram skein)
- [Color A] Medium Teal #66; 1 skein, uses approximately 45 (70, 95, 130, 170, 215) yards
- [Color B] Tango #70; 1 skein, uses approximately 40 (60, 90, 120, 160, 200) yards
- [Color C] Pear #74; 1 skein, uses approximately 45 (70, 95, 130, 170, 215) yards
- [Color D] Fuchsia #320; 1 skein, uses approximately 45 (70, 95, 130, 170, 215) yards
- [Color E] Yellow #338; 1 skein, uses approximately 35 (55, 80, 105, 140, 175) yards

✧ 32–40-inch US #6/4mm circular needle, or size needed to obtain gauge
✧ Optional buttons

Gauge
22 stitches and 34 rows = 4"/10 cm in stockinette stitch.

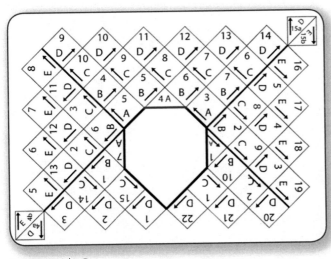

FIGURE 1 Yoke Diagram

BLOCK 5 Cast on 4 (5, 6, 7, 8, 9) stitches; work all rows of end-of-tier rectangle.

RIGHT SLEEVE TIER, COLOR B

BLOCK 6 Beginning- and end-of-tier rectangle.

RIGHT FRONT TIER, COLOR A

BLOCK 7 Right front triangle.

Along edge of Block 6, pick up 4 (5, 6, 7, 8, 9) stitches.

Row 1 (WS): Sl1p, purl across, turn.
Row 2 (RS): Sl1k, knit to last 2 stitches, ssk, turn. 1 st. less.
Repeat rows 1 and 2 until you have 1 stitch; last stitch will be bound off over next picked up stitch.

Triangle complete.

ROUND 2 With Colors B and C, working clockwise (from left to right), follow Chart B on page 11. (Figure 3)

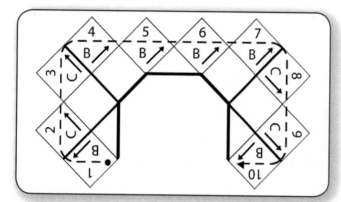

FIGURE 3 Round 2

RIGHT FRONT TIER, COLOR B

BLOCK 1 Slip last stitch from previous round to opposite needle; pick up 4 (5, 6, 7, 8, 9) stitches. Binding off last stitch from previous round over first stitch of this round, continue working end-of-tier rectangle.

RIGHT SLEEVE TIER, COLOR C

BLOCK 2 Beginning-of-tier rectangle.
BLOCK 3 End-of-tier rectangle.

BACK TIER, COLOR B

BLOCK 4 Beginning-of-tier rectangle.
BLOCKS 5–6 Middle-of-tier rectangles.
BLOCK 7 End-of-tier rectangle.

LEFT SLEEVE TIER, COLOR C

BLOCK 8 Beginning-of-tier rectangle.
BLOCK 9 End-of-tier rectangle.

LEFT FRONT TIER, COLOR B

BLOCK 10 Beginning-of-tier rectangle.

ROUND 3 With Colors C and D, working counter-clockwise, follow Chart A on page 10. (Figure 4)

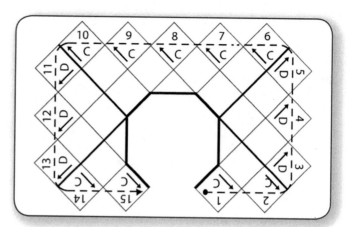

FIGURE 4 Round 3

LEFT FRONT TIER, COLOR C

BLOCK 1 Cast-on rectangle.
BLOCK 2 End-of-tier rectangle.

LEFT SLEEVE TIER, COLOR D

BLOCK 3 Beginning-of-tier rectangle.
BLOCK 4 Middle-of-tier rectangle.
BLOCK 5 End-of-tier rectangle.

BACK TIER, COLOR C

BLOCK 6 Beginning-of-tier rectangle.
BLOCKS 7–9 Middle-of-tier rectangles.
BLOCK 10 End-of-tier rectangle.

RIGHT SLEEVE TIER, COLOR D

BLOCK 11 Beginning-of-tier rectangle.
BLOCK 12 Middle-of-tier rectangle.
BLOCK 13 End-of-tier rectangle.

RIGHT FRONT TIER, COLOR C

BLOCK 14 Beginning-of-tier rectangle.
BLOCK 15 End-of-tier rectangle.

ROUND 4 With Colors D and E, working clockwise, follow Chart B on page 11. (Figure 5)

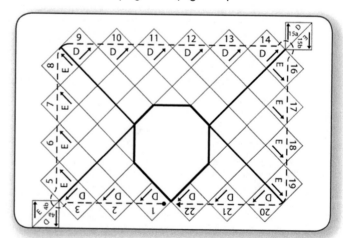

FIGURE 5 Round 4

RIGHT FRONT TIER, COLOR D

BLOCK 1 Cast-on rectangle.
BLOCK 2 Middle-of-tier rectangle.
BLOCK 3 End-of-tier rectangle.
BLOCK 4A Underarm body triangle.

Cast on 1.

Row1 (RS): K1, turn.
Row 2 (WS): Pf&b, turn. 2 sts.
Row 3: Sl1k, k1, turn.
Row 4: Sl1p, pf&b, turn. 3 sts.
Row 5: Sl1k, k2, turn.
Row 6: Sl1p, purl across to last stitch, pf&b, turn. 1 add'l st.
Row 7: Sl1k, knit across, turn.

Repeat rows 6 and 7 until you have 4 (5, 6, 7, 8, 9) stitches.

Row 8 (10, 12, 14, 16, 18): Sl1p, purl across.

Triangle complete; leave at least 12 inch tails for any extra sewing needed under arm with Color D and Color E.

RIGHT SLEEVE TIER, COLOR E

BLOCK 4B Underarm sleeve triangle.

With RS facing, working from right to left, along bottom of Block 4a, the pf&b edge, pick up 4 (5, 6, 7, 8, 9) stitches knitwise. On opposite needle, pull cable as for

beginning-of-tier.

Row 1 (WS): Sl1p, turn.
Row 2 (RS): K1, turn.
Row 3: Sl1p, p1, turn.
Row 4: Sl1k, k1, turn.
Row 5: Sl1p, p2, turn.

Repeat rows 4 and 5, working one additional stitch each pair until all stitches have been purled, ending with sl1p, p3 (4, 5, 6, 7, 8).

Both triangles creating underarm shaping rectangle complete.

BLOCK 5 Middle-of-tier rectangle; stitches are picked up from Block 3.
BLOCKS 6–7 Middle-of-tier rectangles.
BLOCK 8 End-of-tier rectangle.

BACK TIER, COLOR D

BLOCKS 9 Beginning-of-tier rectangle.
BLOCKS 10–13 Middle-of-tier rectangles.
BLOCK 14 End-of-tier rectangle.
BLOCK 15A Underarm bodice triangle; same as Block 4a.

LEFT SLEEVE TIER, COLOR E

BLOCK 15B Underarm sleeve triangle; same as Block 4b.
BLOCK 16 Middle-of-tier rectangle; stitches are picked up from Block 14.
BLOCKS 17–18 Middle-of-tier rectangles.
BLOCK 19 End-of-tier rectangle.

LEFT FRONT TIER, COLOR D

BLOCK 20 Beginning-of-tier rectangle.
BLOCK 21 Middle-of-tier rectangle.
BLOCK 22 End-of-tier rectangle. If working bobble button in next block, do not break yarn.

CARDIGAN BODY INSTRUCTIONS

Note: Congratulations, the yoke is now completed. As you work Round 5, follow the directions to place the sleeve stitches onto stitch holders, and join the Front Tiers to the Back Tier.

ROUND 5 With Color E, working counterclockwise, follow Chart A on page 10. If you are working bobble buttons and/or buttonholes, begin this round.

LEFT FRONT, COLOR E

BLOCK 1 Cast-on rectangle, with bobble buttons (for girls) or buttonholes (for boys) as desired.

Note: Use a long tail cast-on for a finished edge and to have the tail at the best place for sewing in.
Optional bobble Instructions: Using color from previous round, replace stitch in middle of block with the following bobble:

Row 1 (RS): Make 5 by kf&b, kf&b, k.
Row 2 (WS): Sl1k, knit across.
Row 3: Sl1p, purl across.
Row 4: Sl1k, knit across.
Row 5: Sl1p, purl across.

Using left needle, pull second, third, fourth and fifth stitches over first.

Back to original number of stitches; bobble complete.

Optional buttonhole Instructions: In middle of block, k2tog, YO.

Back to original number of stitches; buttonhole complete.

BLOCKS 2–3 Middle-of-tier rectangles.
BLOCK 4 Pick up stitches for middle-of-tier rectangle. Using 5 stitch holders, place working stitches for sleeve blocks onto stitch holders, blocks 19-15b in color E from round 4. Complete middle-of-tier rectangle, attaching to Color D from Block 15a.
BLOCKS 5–10 Middle-of-tier rectangles.
BLOCK 11 Pick up stitches for middle-of-tier rectangle. Place working stitches for sleeve blocks onto stitch holders, blocks 8-4b in color E from round 4. Complete middle-of-tier rectangle, attaching to Color D from Block 4a.
BLOCKS 12–14 Middle-of-tier rectangle.

BLOCK 15 Begin end-of-tier rectangle, with buttonholes (for boys) or buttons (for girls) as desired. For bobble and buttonhole instructions, see Block 1. On next to last row, row 7 (9, 11, 13, 15, 17), bind off as you purl row. Last row omitted. Last stitch will be bound off over first stitch of next round.

ROUND 6 With Color A, working clockwise, follow Chart B on page 11.

BLOCK 1 Beginning-of-tier rectangle, binding off last stitch from previous block over first stitch.
BLOCKS 2–14 Middle-of-tier rectangles.

ROUND 7 With Color B, working counterclockwise, follow Chart A on page 10.

BLOCK 1 Cast-on rectangle, with buttons (for girls) or buttonholes (for boys) as desired.
BLOCKS 2–14 Middle-of-tier rectangles.
BLOCK 15 End-of-tier rectangle with bind-off, with buttonholes (for girls) or buttons (for boys) as desired.

ROUND 8 With Color C, working clockwise, follow Chart B on page 11.

BLOCK 1 Beginning-of-tier rectangle, binding off last stitch from previous block over first stitch.
BLOCKS 2–14 Middle-of-tier rectangles.

ROUND 9 With Color D, working counterclockwise, follow Chart A on page 10.

BLOCK 1 Cast-on rectangle, with buttons (for girls) or buttonholes (for boys) as desired.

BLOCKS 2–14 Middle-of-tier rectangles.

BLOCK 15 End-of-tier rectangle with bind-off, with buttonholes (for girls) or buttons (for boys) as desired.

ROUND 10 With Color E, working clockwise, follow Chart B on page 11.

BLOCK 1 Beginning-of-tier rectangle, binding off last stitch from previous block over first stitch.

BLOCKS 2–14 Middle-of-tier rectangles.

ROUND 11 With Color A, working counterclockwise, follow Chart A on page 10.

BLOCK 1 Cast-on rectangle, with buttons (for girls) or buttonholes (for boys) as desired.

BLOCKS 2–14 Middle-of-tier rectangles.

BLOCK 15 End-of-tier rectangle with bind-off, with buttonholes (for girls) or buttons (for boys) as desired.

ROUND 12 With Color B, working clockwise, follow Chart B on page 11.

BLOCK 1 Beginning-of-tier rectangle, binding off last stitch from previous block over first stitch.

BLOCKS 2–14 Middle-of-tier rectangles.

ROUND 13 With Color C, working counterclockwise, follow Chart A on page 10.

BLOCK 1 Cast-on rectangle, with buttons (for girls) or buttonholes (for boys) as desired.

BLOCKS 2–14 Middle-of-tier rectangles.

BLOCK 15 End-of-tier rectangle with bind-off, with buttonholes (for girls) or buttons (for boys) as desired.

ROUND 14 With Color D, working clockwise, follow Chart B on page 11.

BLOCK 1 Beginning-of-tier rectangle, binding off last stitch from previous block over first stitch. On last row, bind off all stitches.

BLOCKS 2–14 Middle-of-tier rectangles with bind-off.

SLEEVE INSTRUCTIONS

Work each sleeve in same way.

Beginning at bottom of sleeve, pick up stitches from holders.

All rounds will be 5 middle-of-tier rectangles, using Chart A for odd rounds and Chart B for even rounds. Begin with block under arm. Stitches are picked up from the outside point of the blocks, down towards the valley between blocks.

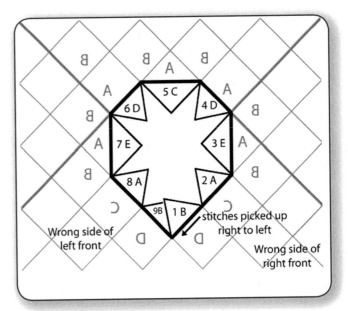

FIGURE 6 *Jester Collar Diagram*

ROUND 1 with Color A, follow Chart A on page 10.

ROUND 2 with Color B, follow Chart B on page 11.

ROUND 3 with Color C, follow Chart A on page 10.

ROUND 4 with Color D, follow Chart B on page 11.

ROUND 5 with Color E, follow Chart A on page 10.

ROUND 6 with Color A, follow Chart B on page 11.

ROUND 7 with Color B, follow Chart A on page 10.

ROUND 8 with Color C, follow Chart B on page 11.

Work middle-of-tier rectangles with bind-offs.

PETER PAN COLLAR INSTRUCTIONS

Starting at left front edge of yoke, with WS facing, using Color A, pick up 36, (45, 54, 63, 72, 81) stitches knitwise, 4 (5, 6, 7, 8, 9) stitches in each of nine center blocks. Note that stitches are picked up knit-wise because WS of yoke is RS of collar. Place 4 stitch markers, 2 at each shoulder. Counting from each neck edge, place marker after 11th (14th , 17th, 20th, 23rd, and 26th) stitches; skip 2 stitches, and place second marker.

Row 1(WS of collar, RS of yoke): Sl1k, knit to first set of markers; slip marker, kf&b, kf&b, slip marker. Knit to second set of markers; slip marker, kf&b, kf&b, slip marker; knit to end.

Change to Color B

Row 2 (RS of collar, WS of yoke): Sl1k, knit across.
Row 3: Sl1k, knit to first set of markers; slip marker, kf&b, k2, kf&b, slip marker. Knit to second set of markers; slip marker, kf&b, k2, kf&b, slip marker; knit to end.

Change to Color C

Row 4: Sl1k, knit across.
Row 5: Sl1k, knit to first set of markers; slip marker, kf&b, k4, kf&b, slip marker. Knit to second set of markers; slip marker, kf&b, k4, kf&b, slip marker; knit to end.

Change to Color D

Row 6: Sl1k, knit across.
Row 7: Sl1k, knit to first set of markers; slip marker, kf&b, k6, kf&b, slip marker. Knit to second set of markers; slip marker, kf&b, k6, kf&b, slip marker; knit to end.

Change to Color E

Row 8: Sl1k, knit across.
Row 9: Sl1k, knit to first set of markers; slip marker, kf&b, k8, kf&b, slip marker. Knit to second set of markers; slip marker, kf&b, k8, kf&b, slip marker; knit to end.

Change to Color A

Row 10: Sl1k, knit across.
Row 11: Sl1k, knit to first set of markers; slip marker, kf&b, k10, kf&b, slip marker. Knit to second set of markers; slip marker, kf&b, k10, kf&b, slip marker; knit to end.
Row 12: Sl1k, knit across, binding off all stitches. After sewing in ends, tack collar down.

JESTER POINT COLLAR INSTRUCTIONS (FIGURE 6)

POINT 1 Starting in first block of right front edge of yoke, with WS facing, using Color B, pick up 4 (6, 6, 8, 8, 10) stitches knitwise. Stitches are picked up knitwise because WS of yoke is RS of collar. Pick stitches up "backwards" from right to left so working yarn will be at front edge of sweater.

Cast on 2 stitches.

Row 1 (in, WS collar, RS sweater): Kf&b, ssk (first stitch cast on with adjacent stitch picked up from neck edge). 3 sts.
Row 2 (out, RS collar, WS sweater): Sl1k, k2, turn.
Row 3: Kf&b, k1, ssk, turn. 4 sts.
Row 4: Sl1k, k3, turn; for doll size, skip to row 17.
Row 5: Kf&b, k2, ssk, turn. 5 sts.
Row 6: Sl1k, k4, turn; for sizes 3–6 mos. & 9–12 mos., skip to row 15.
Row 7: Kf&b, k3, ssk, turn. 6 sts.
Row 8: Sl1k, k5, turn; for sizes 18 mos.–2T & 4–6 yrs., skip to row 13.

Row 9: Kf&b, k4, ssk, turn. 7 sts.
Row 10: Sl1k, k6, turn.
Row 11: Ssk, k4, ssk, turn. 6 sts.
Row 12: Sl1k, k5, turn.
Row 13: Ssk, k3, ssk, turn. 5 sts.
Row 14: Sl1k, k4, turn.
Row 15: Ssk, k2, ssk, turn. 4 sts.
Row 16: S l1k, k3, turn.
Row 17: Ssk, k1, ssk, turn. 3 sts.
Row 18: S l1k, k2, turn.
Row 19: Ssk, ssk. 2 sts.

POINT 2 In next block around yoke, with yoke WS facing edge, using Color A, pick up 4 (6, 6, 8, 8, 10) stitches knitwise. Pick stitches up "backwards" from right to left so working yarn will be next to two stitches from previous point.

Row 0: K2
Row 1–19: Same as Point 1
POINT 3 Same as point 2 with Color E.
POINT 4 Same as point 2 with Color D.
POINT 5 Same as point 2 with Color C.
POINT 6 Same as point 2 with Color D.
POINT 7 Same as point 2 with Color E.
POINT 8 Same as point 2 with Color A.
POINT 9 With Color B, work rows 0–18 same as point 2.

Bind off while working row 19.

FINISHING

Sew in ends. See Appendix, Entrelac Tips, Terms and Techniques, Sewing in Ends, for tips on how to have a neatly finished edge. Wash and block.

Avoiding Mistakes: With entrelac, it is almost impossible to go back and fix mistakes after you have moved on to the next block. Given that the rounds are worked in opposite directions, a mistake made in a block early in one round is then found near the end of the following round. That means either ripping out almost two full rounds of work or creative camouflage. Even though it's tedious, I recount rows and stitches in each block before moving on to the next. If you find you have a tendency to join blocks where you shouldn't, try using a stitch marker to separate the two blocks that are not being joined.

Braided Join: I explain general joining techniques and methods in the section Invisible Joins, below, but this technique from clever Canadian Lorraine L. is my favorite, http://www.youtube.com/watch?v=kHWbKOta02M&nofeather=True

Casting On: (not Provisional Cast-On, covered below) When casting on at an outside edge, I usually use a long-tail cast on. Depending on the slant of the round, I cast on with either my right hand or my left. For counterclockwise rounds (Chart A on page 10), the cast-on occurs on the RS, so I use a standard cast-on using my left hand to cast on stitches onto the right hand needle. For clockwise rounds (Chart B on page 11), the cast-on occurs on the WS, so I turn my work and use a backwards cast-on using my right hand to cast on stitches onto the left hand needle (see Knitting Backwards, below). When casting on with working yarn that is already attached, I use a cable cast-on.

Changing Colors: You will be changing colors every time you turn a corner, so it is essential to find a technique that works well for you. I prefer to use Invisible Joins (see below), except in the final round of my work when I leave long tails to connect the blocks while sewing in ends (see Sewing In Ends, below). If you do not join the yarn as you go, you might want to make a slip knot as you change colors to avoid introducing too much slack at the color change.

E-cord: E-cord, or entrelac cord, is entrelac in the round worked with only two blocks in each round. Working E-cord is not as easy or fast as I-cord, but it does make a very sturdy strap or cord. It may also be used in other ways, as thumbs, ears, etc. For directions, see the purse pattern on page 68.

Gauge: For the patterns in this book, the gauges are given for a flat 4"x4" swatch. For most patterns, an accurate gauge is not required. For the sized patterns, unless you work entrelac with large selvedges, a flat swatch should be sufficient. If you do wish to measure a diagonal entrelac gauge, use the coaster pattern on page 36 for your swatch.

Invisible Joins: You will be changing colors every time you turn a corner, so it is essential to find a technique that works well for you. A Russian join is fast and easy, but I prefer to work a braided join (see Braided Join, above) as it is a little tighter and less noticeable. For either join, it takes a little practice to put it in just the right spot. For the first join, work to the end of the block to where you wish to change colors, mark the spot on your working yarn, and then carefully "tink" or unknit that final row. Now, measure how much yarn will be used for the join, and keep it consistent for all joins. Do not trim the ends until after washing and blocking.

Knitting Backwards: After knitting the front of your work from right to left, you usually turn your knitting and work the back, often purling, again from right to left. When you knit backwards, after knitting the front, you do not turn your work, and instead, knit from left to right. Everything you usually do with your left hand is done with the right, and vice versa, creating a mirror image of how you usually knit. This can be very handy when knitting entrelac as there are so, so many little rows.

Magic Loop: The Magic Loop is a Fiber Trends booklet by Bev Galeskas. Her technique uses one long circular needle to replace double pointed needles.

Mitering (turning) the Corner: This technique may seem odd as you start, but with a little practice, you will get the hang of it. It is important to remember that blocks at each end of an entrelac tier are not standard blocks. The last block in any tier does not attach. The first block of the next tier changes color, and the working stitches are picked up from the block just knit (you will need to pull out loose cable to do that).

Needle Management: Knitting mitered entrelac patterns is much like knitting a circular shawl. At the beginning, there are very few stitches, and by the outer edge, there may be too many stitches to fit on even your longest needle. Fortunately, there are two techniques using circular needles that make this transition possible, Magic Loop (see Magic Loop section, above) and Two Circular Needles, (see Two Circular Needles, below). In general, I start out using the Magic Loop method with the longest needle I can stand. When the piece gets too large, or when I want to flatten it out and admire my work, I switch to Two Circular Needles. When a piece is very long and thin, like a scarf, it is easier to knit one half at a time. The second half is worked onto the first.

Outside Corner Blocks: Standard entrelac blocks are not squares; they are rectangles. When the blocks are surrounded by other entrelac blocks, they are pulled into a more square shape. The outside corner blocks are attached along only one edge, making the rectangular shape more pronounced. The first block worked in the final (bind-off) tier will be short and wide. To mitigate this slightly, you may cast on the stitches, and then slip one cast-on stitch back onto the left needle and immediately knit (ssk) or purl (p2tog) that stitch with the stitch from the block below. This results in two fewer rows. The final block of your bound-off edge will be long and skinny. Work the full number of rows for a regular block to make sure there is enough yarn. HOWEVER, when looking at the final project, you may decide to make this block a row or two shorter. Corner blocks can also be made slightly more square while blocking. Since these blocks will be more prominent than others, it is especially important to use care sewing in ends (see Sewing in Ends, below).

Picking Up Stitches: You will be picking up stitches even more often than changing colors, so be careful with this technique. See Chapter 4, Double Half Stitch Pick Up, on page 19 for an innovative way to have a beautiful transition between blocks.

Provisional Cast-On: I know; I hear you, please say it isn't so! Why does provisionally casting on have such a terrible reputation? It's such a useful technique, and in entrelac you only have to do 4 to 9 stitches at a time. See Chapter 3, Provisional Cast-on, on page 15 for an easy way to cast those stitches directly onto your needle and cable.

Sewing in Ends: To get a nicely finished outside edge, I always sew my tail through the first stitch of the adjacent block of the same color, and then back through my last cast off stitch to tie these blocks together and mimic the look of blocks where the last stitch of one block is cast off over the first stitch of the following block.

Two Circular Needles: Socks Soar on Two Circular Needles is by Cat Bordi. Her technique uses two circular needles to replace double pointed needles.

Yarn Choices: When knitting for children and the kitchen, I like to use washable yarns, cotton or superwash. Of course, the same properties that make them wash well, mean that your ends never self-felt and disappear. It is especially valuable to use an Invisible Join. For the ends that do need to be sewn in, like the outside round, I usually sew in for two full rows

ABBREVIATIONS

[ ]	work instructions within brackets as many times as directed
"	Inch(es)
CC	contrasting color
CCW	counterclockwise
CW	clockwise
dpn(s)	double point needle(s)
k	knit
k2tog	knit 2 stitches together
kf&b	knit into front and back of a single stitch to increase one stitch
mm	millimeter(s)
m1L	with the left hand needle, working front to back, pick up the running thread between two stitches and knit tbl for a left-slanting increase
m1R	with the left hand needle, working back to front, pick up the running thread between two stitches and knit for a right-slanting increase
MC	main color
p	purl
p2tog	purl 2 stitches together
pf&b	purl into front and back of a single stitch to increase one stitch
pm	place marker
RS	right side
sl1k	slip one knitwise
sl1p	slip one purlwise
ssk	slip a stitch knitwise, slip a second stitch knitwise, knit both stitches together tbl
sssk	slip a stitch knitwise, slip a second stitch knitwise, slip a third stitch knitwise, knit all three stitches together tbl
st(s)	stitch(es)
tbl	through the back loop
WS	wrong side
YO	yarn over

DEDICATION

This book is dedicated to my family with thanks for their support during the writing process. First to my husband who not only provided business advice, but also walked to the 7-Eleven more times than I like to admit for milk, eggs and bread when we ran out of food again. To our two lovely daughters, great cheerleaders, who have developed an encouraging way of gently steering me in the right direction. Finally, to my parents, who sacrificed so much to provide an amazing education, culminating in my engineering degree, and then smiled as I left engineering, first to teach, then to be at home, and finally to knit. Of course it was my mom who taught me to knit in the first place.

ABOUT THE AUTHOR

Laura's knitting design and love of teaching have been influenced at every stage of her life. She grew up sewing and knitting a bit with a mother who insisted on meticulous finishes. In college, she majored in engineering, and learned to knit sweaters. After working as a Project Manager in engineering design, she returned to the classroom, teaching high school math and writing and teaching "Introduction to Engineering" for a magnet program. Her knitting, sewing and teaching continued as she married, had children, and moved many times, including to Australia and Brazil. When her family finally settled in Washington, DC, her focus turned to knitting. At first she was primarily knitting mittens for the homeless, but then designed a blanket as a wedding gift, learned to knit lace, and discovered Socks Soar on Circular Needles. Cat Bordi opened her eyes to the possibility of reengineering knitting techniques and möbius! As Laura started pushing her own knitting boundaries, she was also busily teaching the scouts and her daughter's 6th grade class to knit, and developing methods to help friends improve and expand their knitting skills.

In 2012, she created her company, CathedralKnits. To Laura, cathedrals represent some of the cutting edge technology of their time (the Middle Ages), intricate mathematical calculations, exquisite craftsmanship, and the willingness to attempt something incredibly challenging. Many people don't see any of that, just beauty, and that makes them equally happy. Her goals are to push the boundaries of what can currently be knit, and then enthusiastically and engagingly to guide others to their own knitting success. Visit her website at CathedralKnits.com.

ABOUT THE PHOTOGRAPHER

A graduate of RISD, Tanis Gray lives in Alexandria, VA with her green Mechanical Engineer husband, toddler son and lazy pug. Having worked at Martha Stewart, HBO, Focus Features, in the art department in the film and television industries, and a 4-year career as the Yarn Editor at *Vogue Knitting* and co-editor of *Knit.1*, she has been working in the creative field for many years. Tanis has over 350 published knitting designs, and her work has been featured in many major publications and books worldwide, including 12 covers. She also edits other knitting books, photographs knitting books, plans and executes social media for numerous yarn companies and teaches advanced knitting often in and around DC. Tanis has her own regularly-featured TV spot on PBS' *Knitting Daily TV*. Follow her at www.tanisknits.com.

INDEX